THE
COMPACT
GUIDE

T0108422

QUEEN

ELIZABETH II

Rod Green

ANDRE
DEUTSCH

OTHER TITLES IN THE COMPACT GUIDE SERIES

Winston Churchill

The Cold War

DNA

The Elements

The Napoleonic Wars

THIS IS AN ANDRE DEUTSCH BOOK

Text © Andre Deutsch 2018
Design © Andre Deutsch 2019

Originally published in 2018 under the title *Majesty*.
This edition published in 2019 by Andre Deutsch
A division of the Carlton Publishing Group
20 Mortimer Street
London
W1T 3JW

Typeset by JCS Publishing Services Ltd

Printed in Italy

ISBN: 978-0-233-00595-9

C O N T E N T S

INTRODUCTION

There were a number of things that became obvious when researching and writing this book; things that, while they were not previously any kind of secret, neither did they immediately spring to mind when most of us think of the royal family and the House of Windsor.

For the most part we see the ceremonial side of royalty – the Queen and her family smiling and waving from cars or carriages, with police escorts or troops of cavalry escorting them to and from the ribbon-cutting to open a bridge or a civic centre, or all of the glitz and pageantry of a state occasion such as a royal wedding or Trooping the Colour. We see various members of the royal family on TV, making speeches at lunches for business leaders or charity functions, and we see the Queen delivering her government's "Queen's Speech" at the state opening of Parliament, or in a slightly more relaxed setting when she delivers her Christmas broadcast.

What we don't see is all of the work that goes on behind the scenes before events, speeches or broadcasts like these. The army of staff that supports the royal family has to operate like any other business, but unlike any other business their main aim is not to sell their own product or service – their role is far more complex than that. They are not operating in only one sector – they are a multi-national operation that has to take into account not only their own image or "brand" in markets all over the world, but also the intricacies of politics and diplomacy. Their business, with the Queen as CEO, is to further the best interests of the United Kingdom and the Commonwealth.

To do that, the royal family has to protect and maintain the institution of the monarchy. That has never been easy. The House of Windsor was created during the First World War to protect the monarchy and there have been many crises since then that have threatened the stability of the institution. That it has survived is a tribute to the dedication and hard work of all of the senior royals, not only on the international stage, but also at local level, working with people all over the United Kingdom. A good example of this came when Dumfries House, near Cumnock in Ayrshire, was to be sold and its unique collection of art and furniture auctioned off. Prince Charles was determined that it should be saved for the nation and he worked tirelessly to raise the millions needed – even arranging for his own charitable foundation to take on a £20 million loan. He was negotiating a deal when the first of the Chippendale collection was already loaded onto trucks bound for the auction rooms. The house, after extensive renovation, is now a thriving tourist attraction, cultural and education centre, providing local jobs as a "heritage-led regeneration scheme". This was not a government initiative. It was a project spearheaded by the prince.

The members of the royal family often face challenges that only their sense of duty can carry them through. When the Queen talked to survivors and families after the attack on the World Trade Center in New York, the Manchester Arena bombing and the Grenfell Tower disaster in London, the experience was undoubtedly traumatic for her, but any small comfort that she can provide, even if it is only to show people that others are aware and sympathize with their suffering, is hugely important. Her own mother and father provided that comfort during the Second World War, touring areas in London and beyond that were devastated by enemy bombing, and the Queen and her family see it as their duty to shoulder that responsibility today.

There are lighter moments, of course, and the Queen, however serious she may have to be when the moment requires it, has always had a great sense of fun. Anyone who has not seen the video she made with Prince Harry and Barack and Michelle Obama to promote the Invictus Games should give it a look. It's out there on the Internet.

The royal family may live lives of great privilege but the sense of duty that has been instilled in them in the modern era by the incredible dedication of the Queen and Prince Philip has ensured that the Queen's children, grandchildren and great-grandchildren are preparing to carry the House of Windsor forward from its first 100 years for another century and beyond.

Rod Green

CHAPTER ONE

CREATING A NEW DYNASTY

When Queen Victoria died in January 1901, only a year into the new century, the world was changing fast. In the 63 years since she had come to the throne, new inventions and innovations had revolutionized the way that people lived, bringing greater luxury and leisure to the wealthy elite, while impacting enormously on the everyday lives of ordinary people.

Factories where waterwheels had originally powered the machinery had turned to steam power, which meant that new industrial premises need not be built by the banks of a river or stream. This allowed Britain's great manufacturing centres to thrive closer to the city ports from where their produce could be shipped throughout Britain and the empire by rail and sea.

Railways, which had been in their infancy at the beginning of Victoria's reign, now criss-crossed not only her kingdom but also her worldwide empire. The latest steam trains could travel at more than 80mph (130kmh), an unimaginable speed when Britain's first railway line, the Stockton & Darlington Railway, opened in 1825. At that time people had believed that anyone attempting to travel faster than a racehorse could carry you would not be able to breathe. Steam power had also revolutionized travel at sea and ocean liners could now cross the Atlantic in less than six days, a journey that had previously taken twice as long under sail. The world's first coal-fired power station, the Edison Electric Light Station, had been built on Holborn Viaduct in London in 1882, and by the turn of the century electric street lights were widespread throughout central London. Telephones enabled instant communication, automobiles and motorcycles were becoming an ever-more-common sight on the roads and the first cinemas had opened, showing moving pictures.

This was, indeed, a fast-changing world.

A NEWLY URBAN PEOPLE

For the vast majority of the population in turn-of-the-century Britain, fancy new gadgets like cars and telephones were hugely expensive luxuries that they couldn't even dream of owning, yet the impact that these things had on people's lives was massive. During the course of the nineteenth century there had been an exodus of Britain's population from the countryside to the towns, from the fields to the factories, which led to an explosion in the urban population. The stock of available housing in the cities could not grow quickly enough to accommodate the influx of newcomers. Living conditions among the new city-dwellers were often appallingly overcrowded, unhygienic and unhealthy. Working conditions for those in the factories were even harsher. They worked long hours, were poorly paid and there was little regard for the health and well-being of factory personnel, with few safeguards in place when using dangerous machinery.

So why not just move back to the countryside? If life in the city was so dreary and unhealthy, why not turn your back on it and return to the farms? That simply wasn't an option. One of the reasons that those traditional agricultural labourers had moved to the factories was because the labour-intensive farm work was now being done by machines. Steam ploughs, combine harvesters, threshing machines – so many aspects of farm work, which had required numerous farmhands, were now dominated by machines. Steam power had displaced traditional farm labourers into the city factories where, ironically, they worked to build the kinds of machines that had made so much of their previous work in the fields redundant. The Victorian machine age had completed the process of pushing the rural population into the city, changing forever the way that people in Britain lived. There was no way back to the country life because there were no jobs to go back to. To stay in the country meant poverty and starvation. The people had to make city life work better for them.

Of course, with so many people packed so tightly into streets of dingy tenement houses, walking to work each day in the same factories, with the same neighbours, all with the same grievances about the way the workforce was being treated, bold talk among a few about how things needed to change soon grew into loud demands from the many for desperately needed improvements. And their voices were heard – but change came slowly. From 1802 onwards the government introduced numerous pieces of legislation aimed at improving working conditions in the factories. Factory owners were required to ensure that there was sufficient ventilation in their works and also to provide children working for them with two complete sets of clothing. Youngsters aged 14 to 18 were not to work more than 12 hours a day. Those aged between nine and 13 were limited to eight-hour days and those under nine had to go to school. The schools were to be built and paid for by the factory owners.

Gradually, the pace of change and reform picked up. By 1819 workers under 16 were limited to a 72-hour working week and by 1833 children were to work only an eight-hour day, had to have a lunch break and were also required to attend school for at least two hours each day. In 1848 all workers were restricted to a 10-hour day. Of course, sometimes the job and the pay meant more to workers than the regulations, letting factory owners off the hook, but there were official inspectors whose job it was to ensure that the rules were being followed.

Yet the effect of being heard and of seeing how demanding change could actually make a difference – providing that you were properly organized in your endeavours – gave the working-class people of

Britain a feeling of empowerment. Trades unions were formed and grew, spawning a new political party in 1900 – the Labour Party. In the General Election that year, the fledgling Labour Party won only two seats. In the election of 1906 the ruling Conservative Party suffered its worst-ever defeat when it was reduced to 156 MPs. The Liberals made huge gains, giving them 397 seats, and the new Labour Party took 29 seats. Four years later, Labour would win 42 seats. "People power" was on the rise.

KING EDWARD VII – A MONARCH IN TOUCH WITH THE TIMES

What has all this to do with the House of Windsor? Surely the monarchy, especially in the early twentieth century, was well insulated from the travails of the working class? In fact, King Edward VII was far more in touch with the people of Britain than his mother, Queen Victoria, had ever been. The queen had withdrawn from public life to a great degree after the death of her husband, Albert, in 1861. Although she would eventually be seen more regularly by her subjects, with her Golden Jubilee and subsequent Diamond Jubilee helping to restore some of the brilliance to her tarnished popularity, her son, as Prince of Wales, had taken on more of her public duties than might normally have been expected. He visited Canada and the United States of America as well as Egypt and the Middle East – and, of course, he maintained his close family connections with regular trips to royal houses all over Europe. His visits fostered the interests of the nation abroad and his diplomatic skills served to maintain British alliances. The only European monarch he failed to charm was his nephew, Kaiser Wilhelm II of Germany.

Edward VII's royal roadshow was even more active at home. He travelled all over Britain, turning his duties into public occasions. Although he had earned a reputation as a playboy prince in his youth, by the time he was king he had been seen by huge numbers of his subjects and he enjoyed their respect and support. Thousands turned out, dressed in their Sunday best, to wave and cheer when the king and queen visited their town. Even when Edward VII visited Ireland (then still entirely part of the United Kingdom) in 1903, as his mother had done on a rare outing three years previously, he received an enthusiastic welcome. Parading royalty to calm potential political hotspots on the home front was already an established tactic and Irish nationalism was rife – the Sinn Féin ("Ourselves Alone") political party was formed the following year. (Edward VII visited Ireland again in 1904 and 1907.) On 10 July 1906 Newcastle upon Tyne's streets were packed with local people keen to catch a glimpse of the royal couple when the king opened the King Edward VII railway bridge spanning the River Tyne. They rode through the streets in a horse-drawn carriage, acknowledging the cheers of the people. Industrialized cities like Newcastle were the engines driving political change, fuelled by social unrest. Edward VII was undoubtedly well aware of this. The Newcastle visit, like the many others he made, was a great success.

Right up to the end of his life, the king was involved in the politics of his country. When the Liberal Party's David Lloyd George, as Chancellor of the Exchequer, presented his "People's Budget" to Parliament he proposed to increase the taxes on those with high incomes, and even to impose a "supertax" on the richest people in the country. The revenue raised was to be spent on welfare reforms, which included sick pay for workers, free medical treatment and old age pensions. The budget was voted through in the House of Commons but the Conservative Party dominated the House of Lords, which rejected the budget – unsurprisingly, as this attempt at the redistribution of wealth in Britain was going to hit the Conservative aristocracy hardest. The king, however, was in favour. He even agreed, if Prime Minister Herbert Asquith was willing to fight a General Election to ensure that the British public was on the side of the reforms, to create as many new Liberal peers in the House of Lords as were needed to outvote the Conservatives.

That seems unthinkable to us nowadays, when the sovereign – as a constitutional monarch – is expected to remain politically neutral. For Edward VII to be so involved in government was unusual, but not unprecedented. His mother had been known to act as peacemaker between the House of Commons and the House of Lords in the past.

When Edward VII died on 6 May 1910 of respiratory complaints linked to his heavy smoking habit, his son George would reaffirm the commitment regarding the creation of Liberal peers, although subsequent parliamentary reform, which concentrated decision-making power in the elected House of Commons as opposed to the unelected House of Lords, made the strategy all but redundant. The new king, however, would have many other problems to face.

GEORGE V – THE KING WHO SHOULD NEVER HAVE BEEN

Prince George Frederick Ernest Albert was the king who should never have been, a dubious honour that one of his sons would ultimately be obliged to share. The son of the Prince and Princess of Wales, Prince George was born on 3 June 1865 in his parents' home Marlborough House, an eighteenth-century mansion north of The Mall in London. Prince George was third in line to the throne behind his elder brother and his father. He was, therefore, never expected to become king.

A private tutor educated the young prince along with his elder brother, Prince Albert Victor, who was 17 months older. In 1877 both boys were sent off to join the Royal Navy on the training ship HMS *Britannia* in Dartmouth. Their tutor, Canon John Dalton, who was a chaplain to Queen Victoria, was sent with them. HMS *Britannia* had previously been the 121-gun battleship HMS *Prince of Wales*, launched in 1860 and powered by steam engines as well as having sails. Her engines and all but her foremast were removed when she was retired to Dartmouth as a cadet training ship, so the young princes never actually put to sea in *Britannia*. It was two years later that they transferred as midshipmen to HMS *Bacchante* and set off around the world, again accompanied by Canon Dalton.

The *Bacchante* toured the empire, visiting North and South America, the Caribbean and South Africa as well as the Mediterranean, Egypt and Japan, where young George had a dragon tattooed on his arm. Following the three-year cruise of the *Bacchante*, the boys had a spell studying

French and German in Switzerland before Prince Albert continued his studies at Cambridge University and Prince George returned to the Royal Navy, where he served aboard a number of vessels before taking command of the gunboat HMS *Thrush*. During his time in the Royal Navy, Prince George served under his uncle, Prince Alfred, Duke of Edinburgh, who was Commander-in-Chief of the Mediterranean Fleet, based in Malta. While there, George actually proposed marriage to his cousin, Princess Marie, but she turned him down, despite him having the approval of his uncle and his father.

In 1891 Prince George, having been promoted to Commander, was in command of the cruiser HMS *Melamphus* when his career in the Royal Navy came to an abrupt end. An outbreak of influenza known as "Russian flu" became a pandemic that began in late 1889 and lasted for about a year before recurring several times over the following three years. Prince Albert contracted the virus in late 1891 and died in January 1892. Prince George took his brother's place in the line of succession. One day he would be king.

Not only did Prince George step into his brother's shoes as a future king, but he also decided to marry the woman to whom his brother had become engaged – Mary of Teck. Given that their marriage was seen to be such a success, producing six children, there can be little doubt that this union was the result of a genuine romance rather than a marriage of convenience. Prince George certainly took the obligations of marriage more seriously than his father had done. Edward VII had been known to visit brothels in Paris while he was still Prince of Wales, and after he married he conducted a string of affairs – possibly as many as 50 – most of which his wife was aware of and chose to ignore. Unlike his father, Prince George never took a mistress.

MARY – MOTHER OF THE HOUSE OF WINDSOR

While Queen Victoria, with her nine children, can be said to have established a dynasty, Queen Mary is most certainly the mother of the

House of Windsor. In her lifetime she saw the accession of two queens and four kings: one of the kings was her husband and two were her sons. Her royal credentials were, despite being slightly tarnished by her parents, otherwise impeccable.

Queen Mary was born in Kensington Palace, London, on 26 May 1867 as Princess Victoria Mary Augusta Louise Olga Pauline Claudine Agnes of Teck, and known as Princess "May" after the month of her birth. She was the daughter of Princess Mary Adelaide of Cambridge, who was a granddaughter of King George III. Known as "Fat Mary", Mary Adelaide was popular with the general public but could not be said to have had suitors battling for her hand in marriage. By the time she eventually did marry, her cousin Queen Victoria having pulled some strings to arrange a few introductions, Mary Adelaide was 33 years old.

Mary Adelaide's husband was an impoverished minor German noble, Francis, Duke of Teck. He had little or no income of his own and the couple relied upon an allowance of £5,000 a year from the state, their "salary" for performing royal duties. Although that may not sound like a great deal of money today, when the couple married in 1866 the average wage in the UK was less than £45 a year – roughly equivalent to about £3,000 in today's terms. The duke and duchess were, therefore, receiving the equivalent of more than £330,000 from the state. Queen Victoria also ensured that they were given apartments in Kensington Palace and a country house, White Lodge, in Richmond Park. Mary Adelaide's mother, the Duchess of Cambridge, also helped out financially to the tune of about £4,000 a year.

So it was that Princess Mary came to be born in Kensington Palace, the first of her parents' four children. Despite their healthy income and rent-free accommodation, the family's extravagant spending on fine food, expensive clothes and luxurious foreign holidays, as well as the duke's gambling habit, led to them accumulating so much debt in London that in 1883 they were forced to flee the country. They travelled to Italy, spending some time in Florence where the young Princess Mary visited museums and art galleries. Germany and Austria were also on the itinerary of the extended tour, where both the duke and duchess had relatives. Mary Adelaide's father, Prince Adolphus, had been Viceroy of

Hanover and her mother had been Princess Augusta of Hesse-Kassel, so there was a substantial German contingent for the family to visit.

Two years after leaving England, once their debts had subsided, the duke and duchess returned to White Lodge where the young Princess Mary learned from her mother the art of arranging successful social occasions. As she grew older, Princess Mary began to act as a kind of secretary to her mother and may well have come to realize that her family was not quite in the top drawer of royal society – certainly not among the wealthiest of the royals. Mary Adelaide, however, had plans for her daughter that would change all of that.

Mary Adelaide saw Princess Mary as a suitable candidate for marriage to one of her cousin's grandsons – her cousin being Queen Victoria. The queen came to see Princess Mary as an eminently suitable granddaughter-in-law. She was of royal blood and, importantly, had been born in Britain rather than in Europe. That made her a good choice for Albert, Duke of Clarence, who was second in line to the throne behind his father, the Prince of Wales. Albert and Mary became engaged in 1891 but, sadly, Albert died shortly afterwards during an outbreak of influenza.

Queen Victoria, however, was still keen to have Princess Mary as a future queen and offered nothing but encouragement when Mary grew close to her former fiancé's brother, Prince George, Duke of York. The couple were married on 6 July 1893 in the Chapel Royal, St James's Palace. They lived in York Cottage at Sandringham, but also had apartments in St James's Palace until George became Prince of Wales in 1901, when they moved to Marlborough House.

The couple had a loving relationship and a successful marriage, which resulted in six children: Edward, Albert, Mary, Henry, George and John. When her husband ascended the throne in 1910, the new Queen Mary was a huge support. She accompanied him on tours of the empire and India, and now took a greater role in royal duties at home – she and her husband even discussing matters of state. Theirs was a strong partnership.

KING GEORGE V AND "THE GREAT UNREST"

When George became the monarch, as King George V, he was every bit as aware of the social problems facing his subjects as his father had been. In 1901, as Duke of York, he and the duchess had embarked on a tour of the empire on an ocean liner converted for use as a royal yacht, HMS *Ophir*. While they would tour India four years later, the 1901 tour departed from Portsmouth in March, visiting Gibraltar, Malta, Egypt, Aden, Ceylon, Singapore, Australia, New Zealand, Mauritius, South Africa and Canada on a voyage that took them eight months. They covered 45,000 miles (72,400 kilometres), 33,000 of them at sea, setting something of a benchmark for future royal tours. In a speech at Guildhall in London on 5 December, George, by then Prince of Wales, said:

> No one who had the privilege of enjoying the experiences which we have had during our tour could fail to be struck with one all-prevailing and pressing demand – the want of population. Even in the oldest of our colonies there were abundant signs of this need. Boundless tracts of country yet unexplored, hidden mineral wealth calling for development, vast expanses of virgin soil ready to yield profitable crops to the settlers. And these can be enjoyed under conditions of healthy living, liberal laws, free institutions, in exchange for the overcrowded cities and the almost hopeless struggle for existence, which, alas, too often is the lot of many in the old country.
>
> But one condition, and one only, is made by our colonial brethren, and that is: "Send us suitable emigrants!" I would go further, and appeal to my fellow-countrymen at home to prove the strength of the attachment of the motherland to her children by sending to them only of her best.

As King George V, therefore, he was perfectly acquainted with "the lot of many in the old country". In preparation for his accession, George had been shown state papers by his father, so he had learned

David Lloyd George: Man of the People

Although he was Welsh and brought up as a Welsh-speaker, David Lloyd George was actually born in Manchester, on 17 January 1863, where his father, William George, was working as a teacher. When David was only a couple of months old, William and his wife, Elizabeth, took David and his older sister, Mary Ellen, to live in Pembrokeshire. They bought a farm but William died in 1864 and Elizabeth, by then pregnant with a second son, William, took her children to live with her brother in Llanystumdwy, Caernarvonshire (now Gwynedd).

It was in Llanystumdwy that David first went to school and his uncle, Richard Lloyd, encouraged him to study hard. Tutors helped him with French and Latin in order that he could train as a solicitor. When he qualified, David set up his own practice, his younger brother eventually joining him. Again with his uncle's encouragement, David took an avid interest in politics, becoming Liberal MP for Caernarvon in 1890. Out of respect, David eventually added his uncle's surname to his own name, becoming David Lloyd George, most often referred to as Lloyd George.

His sharp wit and intelligence made him formidable in debate and Lloyd George quickly scaled the political ladder, becoming President of the Board of Trade in 1905 and Chancellor of the Exchequer in 1908. As Chancellor, he declared war on poverty, taxing the rich to pay for welfare reforms to help the poor. He became prime minister in 1916, the first and only Welshman ever to do so, his energy and dynamism helping him to lead a coalition government through the darkest years of the First World War.

After the war, his Liberal/Conservative coalition party won a landslide election victory but the subsequent economic depression and a scandal involving peerages being "sold" for large sums of money intended to boost Liberal Party funds, or perhaps even to help fund a completely new political party, led to his downfall. He resigned as prime minister in 1922, although he remained active in politics and was created 1st Earl Lloyd-George of Dwyfor in 1944. He died the following year.

Lloyd George had married Margaret Owen in 1888 and the couple had five children, although he is known to have had a number of extra-marital relationships. Margaret died in 1941 and two years later Lloyd George married Frances Stevenson, who had worked for him in various roles for over 30 years.

about the governance of the country and the problems Britain faced. Those problems manifested themselves in a most obvious way when, despite the Liberal Party reforms that were to become the foundation of the Welfare State in Britain, industrial unrest caused havoc across the country from the very beginning of George's reign. The period from 1910 to 1914 would come to be known as "The Great Unrest".

In January 1910 the Durham Miners' Union came out on strike in protest at the way new shift patterns were being imposed on the workforce. With 130,000 members, it was the biggest union in the country and the miners' decision to strike was symptomatic of feelings throughout the rest of the industry. Later the same year, striking Welsh miners clashed with police, who were supported by troops, in what became known as the Tonypandy Riots. Around 80 police officers and 500 strikers were injured, with one miner dying from head wounds. In 1911 there was a general transport strike in Liverpool involving dockers, railway workers and seamen. There were mass demonstrations and mounted police charged a crowd of 85,000 protestors, causing 350 injuries. Home Secretary Winston Churchill deployed troops in Liverpool and there was outrage when they opened fire on a crowd, wounding 13 and killing two. In Llanelli, Wales, in August 1911, striking railway workers attempted to stop a train being run by strike-breakers. They succeeded in boarding the train and damping down the boiler, forcing the train to a halt. Troops who were following on behind were diverted into a cutting and besieged by angry protesters. The soldiers were ordered to fire warning shots toward the crowd, but two local men were shot dead. There followed a riot in which business premises were attacked and four more people died when a railway carriage carrying munitions was blown up. The government ordered the company-owners to enter into negotiations with the strikers and the workers' demands were met at a point that the *London Daily News* of 12 August described as "the brink of civil war". The king sent a telegram to the President of the Board of Trade saying "Rejoice to hear that railway strike is at an end" and congratulating all concerned.

From Clydeside, where 11,000 workers in the Singer Sewing Machine Company's factory went on strike, to garment workers in London and confectionery workers in Bristol, people were demanding change, fair pay and better conditions. In the national miners' strike of 1912, nearly one million miners were involved. Nothing ran without coal – ships, trains, factories, power stations and domestic homes all needed coal. The country was in turmoil and there was real concern that the Marxists, socialists, republicans, trade unionists and a plethora of other political activists could turn industrial unrest into outright revolution. Then, in 1914, Britain went to war with Germany.

THE FOUNDING OF A DYNASTY

The king had, no doubt, believed that the war would be a short-lived confrontation. After all, for generations his family had been building a network of monarchies across Europe, from Russia and Norway all the way to Spain. Eight of Queen Victoria's nine children had married into other European royal families. Cousins married cousins in order to keep ancient titles in the family, along with the land, wealth, power and influence that accompanied them. King George V was first cousin to Tsar Nicholas II of Russia and Kaiser Wilhelm II of Germany. As well as maintaining the power and wealth of the European royal web, the arranged marriages were supposed to have helped to avoid the kind of war that was now raging. The heads of state were, after all, family.

The family connections, however, became a problem for the king as the war progressed. The death toll from the trenches and the hideous injuries of the wounded repatriated to Britain created a wave of anti-German sentiment throughout the country. On 13 May 1915 the front page of the *Daily Mirror* showed pictures of anti-German riots in London's East End, where business premises owned by Germans, or anyone with a German name, had been attacked and looted. Similar scenes were played out in other cities across the country. At the Royal Exchange in the City of London, a rally voted overwhelming for the resolution that "All Germans, whether naturalised or not, must go".

The king and queen visited factories and dockyards to help boost morale, but the queen also took on visits of her own. She spoke to wounded servicemen in hospital and even toured the makeshift shrines that had sprung up in the streets of London's East End, where locals honoured loved ones who had been killed. The queen added her own posies to the floral tributes. George V and his queen were desperate to be seen supporting the British people, and seemed to be as popular as ever, but they could not ignore the rising tide of anti-German vitriol. And what was the British royal family if not German?

King George V was the grandson of Queen Victoria, who was the granddaughter of King George III, who was also King of Hanover. Victoria's mother was Princess Victoria of Saxe-Coburg-Saalfeld. Victoria married Prince Albert of Saxe-Coburg and Gotha (her cousin) and Victoria's son, King Edward VII, married Princess Alexandra of Denmark. Alexandra's mother, Louise of Hesse-Kassel, was German and her father, Prince Christian of Schleswig-Holstein-Sonderburg-Glücksburg, was Danish. King George V had married Princess Mary of Teck, whose father was German.

The British royal family's name was, of course, from Prince Albert – Saxe-Coburg-Gotha. The anti-German feeling in the country made that uncomfortable enough, but on 13 June 1917 the name became an unbearable burden, one that it was feared could bring down the monarchy.

That morning London was hit by an air raid. There had been raids before, the giant Zeppelin airships having bombed the capital as well as other cities and ports, but this was the first daylight raid by German aeroplanes and that meant those on the ground could clearly see the black crosses on the wings of the bombers. There was no such thing as precision bombing at that time. Although there were rudimentary bombsights to aim the weapons, the bombing was so imprecise as to be indiscriminate. The raid left 432 people injured and caused 162 deaths, including 18 children who died when North Street School in Poplar, East London, was hit.

The German aircraft were Gotha bombers, named after the city in Thuringia where the company that manufactured them was based – the same city from which the British royal family took its name. Those who were suffering from the aerial onslaught had every right to ask why these German bombers, dealing death from the sky and massacring His Majesty's subjects, had the same name as the king. The situation was intolerable. The king and the government agreed that something had to change and, in order to protect the monarchy, the change had to be in the name of the royal family.

Lord Stamfordham, the king's private secretary, was tasked with finding suggestions that would be acceptable to both George V and the government. Plantagenet was suggested, as was Tudor and Stuart, but these were all tainted in some way by historical events. Finally, Stamfordham came up with the solution, inspired by the very place in which he was sitting at his desk – Windsor. The name had no foreign associations and was as solidly English as the famous castle. The king liked it, the government liked it, and on 17 July 1917 a Royal Proclamation was issued, which stated:

WHEREAS We, having taken into consideration the Name and Title of Our Royal House and Family, have determined that henceforth Our House and Family shall be styled and known as the House and Family of Windsor:

And whereas We have further determined for Ourselves and for and on behalf of Our descendants and all other the descendants of Our Grandmother Queen Victoria of blessed and glorious memory to relinquish and discontinue the use of all German Titles and Dignities:

And whereas We have declared these Our determinations in Our Privy Council:

Now, therefore, We, out of Our Royal Will and Authority, do hereby declare and announce that as from the date of this Our Royal Proclamation Our House and Family shall be styled and known as the House and Family of Windsor, and that all the descendants in the male line of Our said Grandmother Queen Victoria who are subjects of these Realms, other than female descendants who may marry or may have married, shall bear the said Name of Windsor.

Former prime minister Lord Rosebery wrote to Lord Stamfordham to congratulate him on his stroke of genius, and saying, "Do you realise that you have christened a dynasty?" It was the beginning of a new era, but although King George V's brand-new Windsor dynasty had shaken off the shackles of its aristocratic German past there were constitutional crises and sorely testing times yet to come.

DECLINE OF THE EUROPEAN MONARCHIES

The reign of George V was marked by the rise of communism, socialism and the Irish Republican Army as well as the gradual decline of the British Empire. He watched as some of the great monarchies of Europe had power wrested from their grasp; he watched as his cousin Wilhelm II fled from Germany into exile in Holland; he watched as his cousin Nicholas II was deposed in Russia and then murdered along with his family. There had been a chance to offer asylum to the tsar and his family, allowing them to settle in Britain, but George V had decided against it. Political militants in Britain had celebrated the overthrow of the tsar, whom they saw as a tyrant oppressing the Russian people. To bring the Romanov family to Britain might have fuelled the fires of discontent and led to the end of the British monarchy as well. George V may have believed that another country, another part of the Europe-wide royal family network, would offer the Romanovs a home. In the end, they went nowhere and the king was horrified by their fate. He subsequently ensured that the last of the Romanovs, including his cousin Xenia Alexandrovna, her family and a contingent of Russian aristocrats, were rescued from the Crimea in March 1919. The Royal Navy battleships HMS *Marlborough* and HMS *Lord Nelson* carried them to safety and Xenia and her family did eventually settle in England.

George V also ensured the safety of Emperor Charles I of Austria: a detachment of guards led by a British Army officer escorted the emperor's family to Switzerland and the Royal Navy subsequently transported them to exile in Madeira. In 1922 George V was also responsible for his cousins Prince Andrew and Princess Alice, along with their family

Kaiser Wilhelm II: The Last Emperor of Germany

Born in the Crown Prince's Palace in Berlin on 27 January 1859, Friedrich Wilhelm Viktor Albert was the son of Prince Frederick William of Prussia and Victoria, the eldest daughter of Britain's Queen Victoria. The birth was a difficult one, leaving him with a withered left arm that he contrived to hide in public, and in photographs, throughout his life.

The young Prince Wilhelm went to school in Kassel and when he finished his studies there in 1877, Queen Victoria rewarded her oldest grandchild with the Order of the Garter. He went on to study law and politics at university before being commissioned as an officer in the Guards to complete a Prussian military education.

Wilhelm became German Emperor and King of Prussia on 15 June 1888 at the age of 29. Within two years, the kaiser had dismissed the German Chancellor, Otto von Bismarck, in an attempt to rule as well as reign. His support of Austria against Serbia following the assassination of his friend, Archduke Franz Ferdinand of Austria, led, through treaties and alliances between other European nations, including Russia, to the nightmare of the First World War.

Wilhelm II had long held the belief that the British were intent on making him their enemy. In an interview with the *Daily Telegraph* in 1908, he said that the British were "mad as March hares" and that he wanted to be friends with Britain but, "The prevailing sentiment among large sections of the middle and lower classes of my own people is not friendly to England." This caused offence not only in Britain, but also at home. Six years later he was convinced that his cousins, King George V in Britain and Tsar Nicholas II in Russia, wanted to wage a "war of annihilation" against Germany.

After four years of war, there were mutinies among the military and Wilhelm II was forced to flee into exile in Holland in November 1918, eventually taking with him dozens of railway wagons packed with furniture, paintings and other items destined for his country mansion in Doorn. The former empress, Augusta, whom Wilhelm had married in 1881 and with whom he had had seven children, died at Doorn in 1921. The following year, 63-year-old Wilhelm married 34-year-old Princess Hermine Reuss of Greiz and the couple were together constantly until his death in 1941.

(including the infant Prince Philip), being rescued from Greece aboard HMS *Calypso*. He and the British government did everything they could to avoid the Romanov tragedy ever being repeated.

At home, King George V and Queen Mary continued to enjoy the support of the majority of the population. Although they did not indulge in the casual "walkabout" meet-and-greet sessions pioneered by their granddaughter, on official visits to towns all over Britain they met more of their subjects than their predecessors had ever done. George V also had a good degree of respect for the ordinary people of Britain. During the General Strike of 1926, one aristocratic mine-owner, Lord Durham, responded to the king's expression of sympathy for the miners by referring to them as "a damned lot of revolutionaries". The king retorted that he should "try living on their wages before you judge them".

There were street parties all over Britain to celebrate his Silver Jubilee in 1935, but by then the king was in increasingly poor health, suffering from a variety of ailments related to his heavy smoking habit. He died at Sandringham on 20 January 1936, aged 70.

T H E   M O N A R C H Y

I N   C R I S I S

During the reign of George V, Europe was plunged into political turmoil that, by the mid-1930s, many in Britain saw as a prelude to another war that would engulf the continent. As early as 1930 Winston Churchill, no longer in government but still a Member of Parliament, warned the Foreign Office that Adolf Hitler, whose Nazi Party was fast gaining ground in Germany, was not to be trusted. Although Hitler claimed to have no intention of waging another war, Churchill wrote: "I, however, am convinced that Hitler, or his followers, will seize the first available opportunity to resort to armed force."

By 1934, as Hitler rapidly expanded his country's military capabilities, George V remarked to Germany's ambassador in London, Leopold von Hoesch, who was not a supporter of Hitler, that Germany was becoming "the peril of the world". Gone was the forlorn hope the king had held prior to the First World War that the European royal family network might be able to use its influence to avert a war. They had not been able to do so in 1914 and had even less influence in the 1930s.

When the Spanish Civil War began in 1936, 27 countries, including Germany and Italy, signed a non-intervention agreement, yet Hitler and Italy's fascist dictator Benito Mussolini sent military aid to the nationalist, widely seen as fascist, General Francisco Franco. The German Condor Legion, using German tanks and German aircraft manned by German personnel, trained with and fought alongside Franco's forces.

On the other side of the world, British, French, Dutch and American territories were under threat by Japan, which went to war with China in 1937. American embargoes of oil and other essential goods in retaliation for Japanese aggression meant that some form of conflict in the Far East was becoming almost inevitable. In September 1939 war broke out in Europe and a year later Japan signed the Tripartite Pact in Berlin, agreeing a military alliance with Germany and Italy. Hungary, Romania and Bulgaria also subsequently became signatories to the pact.

Three British kings watched the world's gradual descent into war: George V, his successor Edward VIII and Edward VIII's successor George VI. The situation should have involved only two kings, but the death of King George V in 1936 led to a crisis in the British monarchy that needed an urgent resolution if the nation was to be prepared for what was to come.

EDWARD VIII – THE UNCROWNED KING

London's rain-lashed streets lay sombre and mournful under a leaden sky on 28 January 1936 as the funeral procession of King George V left Westminster Hall. The king's coffin, borne on a gun carriage drawn by naval gun crews, was draped in the royal standard with the monarch's ceremonial symbols of power – the orb, sceptre and crown – placed on top. Alongside them was the only floral tribute to be seen in the whole procession, a cross of flowers from his wife, Queen Mary.

During the time the king's body had been lying in state at the hall, 300,000 people had come to pay their respects. The largest crowd that had, at that time, ever been seen on the streets of the capital now braved the miserable weather, hundreds of thousands of people standing in utter silence as the procession made its way from Westminster into Hyde Park on its way to Paddington Station. From there George V would travel to his final resting place in St George's Chapel, Windsor Castle.

Queen Mary travelled in the procession in a black carriage accompanied by her sister-in-law, Queen Maud of Norway; her daughter Mary, Princess Royal; and Elizabeth, Duchess of York. Following the gun carriage on foot was Queen Mary's eldest son, King Edward VIII, with his three brothers walking a few paces behind. The procession also included five European kings, heads of state, ambassadors, high-ranking military officers from all over the world, squadrons of cavalry, scores of officers and men from the Royal Navy, the Royal Air Force and the British Army, all marching at a solemn, measured pace with their arms by their sides.

A state funeral was the kind of pomp and pageantry that is such an integral part of the British monarchy – the kind of ceremony that the British can stage in London better than anyone else in any city in the world. The next event of its kind should have been the far more joyous occasion of the coronation of King Edward VIII, but that was never to happen.

Edward VIII had been born Edward Albert Christian George Andrew Patrick David on 23 June 1894. The first three of his names were family names and the last four were the patron saints of England, Scotland, Ireland and Wales. Those close to him knew him as David. As a child he was privately tutored, before going to Osborne Naval College. He served for several months as a midshipman aboard the battleship HMS *Hindustan* in 1910, the year in which he also became Prince of Wales. Following a brief period at Oxford University, where all he appeared to learn was how to play polo, the prince joined the Grenadier Guards in 1914, hoping for active service. The government refused to allow the prince, now first in line to the throne, anywhere near the battlefront, but he defiantly visited the trenches whenever he could and the sight of the prince seemingly sharing their plight made him popular among the troops.

Popularity was something that the Prince of Wales never lacked. He frequently deputized for his father, as preparation for becoming king, throughout the 1920s and undertook many trips to different parts of the empire, even buying a ranch in Alberta, Canada, in 1919. While on an official tour in Barbados in 1920, he revealed a racist streak when he wrote to his married lover, Freda Dudley Ward, saying, "I don't take much to the coloured population who are revolting." He also wrote to Mrs Dudley Ward from Australia, describing the indigenous Australians he had met as being the "most revolting form of living creatures" and "the nearest thing to monkeys I've ever seen".

The public persona of the Prince of Wales was, however, completely different. He was slim and handsome, a fashion trend-setter, and seen as the world's most eligible bachelor, on a par with any movie star of the day. In 1927 the hit song "I've danced with a man, who's danced with a girl, who's danced with the Prince of Wales" was written about him. In private, the prince conducted a number of affairs with married women, including Lady Furness and, from early 1934, Wallis Simpson. Simpson was an American who had divorced her first husband, but was still married to her second. King George V was furious with his son about this inappropriate relationship and is reported to have said, "After I am dead, the boy will ruin himself in twelve months."

When George V died in 1936, the Prince of Wales acceded to the throne, taking the regnal name Edward VIII. Prime Minister Stanley Baldwin quickly became concerned about the king's behaviour. Although he took to the work with apparent enthusiasm, it was soon clear that state papers were not being looked at properly or kept secure at Fort Belvedere, Edward VIII's country house in Windsor Great Park. There was concern that the king's friends might even have access to them, including Mrs Simpson, who was an immediate, urgent problem. Edward VIII declared that he would marry Mrs Simpson, which would not only have been socially unacceptable at the time but which also posed a constitutional problem. As king, Edward VIII was head of the Church of England, which did not allow divorcees to remarry while a previous spouse was still living. Both of Mrs Simpson's husbands were still alive. The British legal system would also not have recognized Mrs Simpson's first divorce, making her second marriage bigamous, let alone any third marriage. The government informed the king that it was not possible for him to marry Wallis Simpson, that the marriage would not be legal and that it was unacceptable not only at home but also in the Dominions of the Commonwealth of Nations and dependent British territories around the world, putting the future of the monarchy in jeopardy.

When Edward VIII's dilemma became public knowledge, some elements of the British press lent him their support while others were most definitely against him. So it was with the general public. There were those who believed the king should be able to marry whoever he liked, and those for whom Mrs Simpson was totally unacceptable. When Mrs Simpson's divorce proceedings began in October 1936, the king was left in no doubt that his government would resign if he attempted to marry her. Edward VIII's only option, if he wanted to marry Wallis Simpson, was to abdicate. His younger brother would become king and Edward would be able to live the rest of his life with the woman he loved, although he would not be able to do so in the United Kingdom. In the end, that was the route that he chose to take. He signed the "Instrument of Abdication", which was witnessed by his three brothers, on 10 December 1936, becoming the only British monarch ever to have voluntarily given up the throne.

A NEW ROYAL FAMILY

It fell to Edward VIII's younger brother, Albert, Duke of York, affectionately known as Bertie, now to become the country's head of state. Born Albert Frederick Arthur George on 14 December 1895, the duke had long lived in the shadow of his older brother. He was not the suave, fashionable, confident playboy that Edward VIII was. He was shy and withdrawn. He had struggled with a severe stammer as a child, an affliction that he never completely conquered, and had suffered with "knock knees", resulting in him having to wear humiliating, painful leg braces for a time. He was a sickly child, plagued with stomach problems, and easily provoked to both tears and tantrums.

Despite these problems, Prince Albert attended naval college and proceeded to join the Royal Navy as a midshipman, serving on the battleship HMS *Collingwood* at the Battle of Jutland during the First World War and even qualifying as a pilot with the RAF in 1919.

Although he was led somewhat astray by his older brother when he began seeing the married Sheila, Lady Loughborough, a friend of his brother's married lover Freda Dudley Ward, Prince Albert was brought back in line by his father and on 8 July 1920, at the RAF ball at the Ritz Hotel in London, he met the woman who would become his wife. Elizabeth Bowes-Lyon, then 19 years old, was from an aristocratic Scottish family and Prince Albert claimed that he fell in love with her when they danced that night. Lady Elizabeth was not so sure. In a letter to Beryl Poignand, her former governess and most intimate confidante, she described Prince Albert as "quite a nice youth". The prince, by now Duke of York, persevered over the course of the next three years, proposing and being turned down twice before Lady Elizabeth finally agreed to marry him.

The couple were married on 26 April 1923 at Westminster Abbey and lived at 145 Piccadilly, London, a mansion house that looked out across Green Park toward Buckingham Palace. The Duke and Duchess of York began to take on more and more public duties and visited Kenya, Uganda, Sudan and Aden, although public speaking was a trial for the duke, who continued to suffer with his stammer. With the help of Elizabeth and speech therapist Lionel Logue, he eventually learned how to control the impediment, a struggle that featured in the 2010 movie *The King's Speech*.

On 21 April 1926 the duke and duchess's first child was born. Princess Elizabeth Alexandra Mary came into the world at 17 Bruton Street in Mayfair, London, the town house of the Duchess of York's father, the Earl of Strathmore. Before baby Elizabeth was a year old, her parents embarked on an official tour to Australia, leaving Princess Elizabeth with her grandparents. They missed her first birthday but returned with an estimated three tons of toys that had been given to them on the tour. Some were kept, but most went to children in hospital.

Young Elizabeth was a great favourite of her grandfather, George V, who lavished affection on her in a way that he had never done with his sons. He spent time with her, especially at his stud, inspiring Elizabeth's enduring passion for horses. Struggling to pronounce her own name as a toddler, the best she could manage was "Lilibet", the name that she continued to use with close friends and relatives for the rest of her life.

Princess Elizabeth's sister, Princess Margaret Rose, was born on 21 August 1930 at her mother's ancestral home, Glamis Castle in Scotland. Princess Margaret soon developed a character entirely different to that of her elder sister. She loved to be the centre of attention, was a confident singer and delighted everyone with her impersonations. Princess Elizabeth, on the other hand, was eager to please, polite and neat. The toy horses stabled on the landing outside the girls' room on the top floor at 145 Piccadilly were always well groomed and when the princesses were taught to ride, Elizabeth took a keen interest in how the horses were fed, their saddles and tack.

In 1932 the family moved into the Royal Lodge in Windsor Great Park as a weekend home. Previously they had used White Lodge in Richmond Park, which offered far less privacy because Richmond Park is open to the public. On her sixth birthday, the people of Wales presented Princess Elizabeth with a house of her own. "Y Bwthyn Bach" ("The Little House") was a child's playhouse that had featured at the *Daily Mail* Ideal Home Exhibition. It was re-erected in the shadow of the Royal Lodge, complete with its thatched roof, miniature furniture and household appliances. As a child's playhouse, the rooms were not high enough for adults to stand in, but generations of royal youngsters were to enjoy playing there.

The duke and duchess would not contemplate sending their girls off to school, enjoying a far closer family relationship than most other royals or, indeed, many families of the aristocracy at the time, when the accepted practice was that children should be brought up by nannies and any contact should be at the parents' convenience. The princesses did have a governess, Marion Crawford, a 24-year-old Scot whom Princess Elizabeth nicknamed "Crawfie". Rather than the girls going to school, their grandmother, Queen Mary, stipulated the subjects that they should study, majoring on history, and Crawfie took them through their lessons, although other tutors would later be involved.

The Yorks' family life was thrown into turmoil with the abdication of Edward VIII. The Duke of York, having never wanted the throne, became King George VI and Elizabeth, whose hesitation in agreeing to marry the young man she had known as "Prince Bertie" was partly due to her trepidation about becoming a "royal", was now his queen. When Princess

Elizabeth saw a letter sitting on a hall stand addressed to Her Majesty the Queen, she is reported to have said: "That's Mummy now, isn't it?"

The 10-year-old princess was also well aware that this now meant that, one day, she would become queen. When she explained that to her sister, Princess Margaret's reaction was, "Well poor you!" Both girls had seen how completely overwhelming the responsibilities of the monarch were, with endless public duties, official functions and the oppressive attention of the press.

The new royal family moved into Buckingham Palace and on 12 May 1937, the day that had been planned for his brother's coronation, the king and queen were crowned at Westminster Abbey. The princesses attended the ceremony, witnessing the full majesty and excitement of a British royal ceremonial celebration. The overcast skies could not dull the colour or sparkle of the procession through London, where grandstands had been built, buildings had been decorated with banners and flags, and hundreds of thousands thronged the streets. This time the crowd was far from silent, their cheers drowning out the military bands as regiments of troops from all over the Commonwealth, mounted and on foot, marched not with their arms by their sides, but with a swagger. So many were there that the procession from the abbey to Buckingham Palace stretched for two-and-a-half miles (four kilometres). The loudest cheers of all were for the gold state coach and for when the king and queen, with the princesses, appeared on the balcony at Buckingham Palace to wave to the crowds. While their parents wore their ceremonial regalia, the girls each had an identical crown that had been specially made for them.

THE COMING OF WAR

With Hitler's growing belligerence threatening to plunge Europe into war, the king and queen paid a state visit to France in July 1938 to demonstrate solidarity between the two countries. As the nation's figureheads, they also travelled extensively throughout Britain, with an exhausting round of engagements all over the country, including a Girl Guides' parade at Windsor Castle, where the princesses reviewed massed

Franklin Delano Roosevelt: An Inspirational Leader

Widely regarded as the greatest US president of the modern era, and frequently listed as one of the all-time top three, along with George Washington and Abraham Lincoln, FDR, as he came to be known, was born in Hyde Park, New York, into the wealthy Roosevelt family, on 30 January 1882. Theodore Roosevelt, a distant cousin, became President of the USA when FDR was eight years old.

Roosevelt studied at Harvard College and Columbia Law School, then became a lawyer in New York. He married another distant cousin, Eleanor Roosevelt, in 1905 and the couple had six children, although Roosevelt had a number of extra-marital relationships. In 1910 Roosevelt entered politics, campaigning hard to become New York State Senator. He was James M. Cox's running mate when they lost out to Warren Harding in the 1920 presidential elections and the following year he contracted an illness, believed to be polio, which left him paralysed from the waist down. Roosevelt struggled through years of treatment to regain his fitness, ultimately managing to walk a few steps using leg braces. In public and in photographs he made every effort to hide his reliance on a wheelchair as he returned to politics, becoming Governor of New York in 1928 and US President in 1932.

The United States of America was gripped by the Great Depression when Roosevelt came into office and it was his famous New Deal plan that provided relief for the unemployed, promoted economic recovery and introduced reforms in banking and finance. Roosevelt was re-elected in 1936 and 1940, becoming the only president ever to serve more than two terms. Although the USA remained neutral during the first two years of the Second World War, Roosevelt pushed for preparations to be made for the USA to enter the war and for military aid to be sent to Britain. Following the Japanese attack on Pearl Harbor in December 1941, he led the USA through the war years and was re-elected for a third time in 1944. He died on 12 April 1945, aged 63, a month before the German surrender and four months before the atomic bombs dropped on Hiroshima and Nagasaki brought about the Japanese surrender.

ranks of Guides dressed in their own uniforms. The Buckingham Palace Guide Company had been formed, mainly recruiting the daughters of palace employees, to give the princesses some semblance of a normal life.

Joseph Stalin: Hero and Villain

Joseph Vissarionovich Dzhugashvili (Stalin was a pseudonym he later adopted when writing articles), the man who was to lead the Union of Soviet Socialist Republics (USSR), or Soviet Union, during the Second World War and into the Cold War, was born on 18 December 1878, the son of a Georgian cobbler. He was educated at the Theological Seminary in Tiflis (Tbilisi) from 1894, at which time he became involved with the emerging Marxist movement, finally quitting the seminary in 1899.

Stalin joined the Marxist Russian Social Democratic Labour Party. He also led a gang that committed robberies to raise funds for the Bolshevik movement, even kidnapping (for ransom) the children of wealthy parents. He was arrested and imprisoned several times, but when the Bolsheviks came to power in the 1917 revolution, Stalin was at the head of the government, supporting its leader, Vladimir Lenin. Before the civil war ended in 1923 it is estimated that at least 1.5 million combatants and up to eight million civilians had died.

Ruthless in dealing with enemies of the new state during the civil war, Stalin maintained that reputation when he took control after the death of Lenin in 1924. Between 1934 and 1939, hundreds of thousands of politicians, military officers and intellectuals were imprisoned or executed without trial. Estimates put the death toll during the Great Purges between 1936 and 1938 at more than 600,000, with mobile gas vans even being used to execute prisoners.

Stalin signed a non-aggression pact with Germany and participated in the invasion of Poland in 1939, although Germany ultimately invaded the Soviet Union in 1941. The Soviet Red Army eventually turned the tide, but it is estimated that over 26 million Soviets died before the Red Army took Berlin in May 1945. Stalin subsequently reneged on agreements with his Western allies regarding Poland and countries in Eastern Europe, leading to the East–West stand-off of the Cold War.

Stalin died on 5 March 1953. He had been married twice, his first wife having shot herself after arguing with him over politics. He had three children: his two sons, Yakov and Vasily, both served in the military and Yakov died during the Second World War; his daughter, Svetlana, defected to the USA in the 1960s and she later lived in England, where she became a British citizen.

To many in the former Soviet Union, Stalin remains one of the founders of the nation and a heroic war leader, but to others his ruthless repression of his own people makes him the most villainous dictator of all time.

Adolf Hitler: The Politics of Hate

The man who would change the face of Europe, Adolphus Hitler, was born in Austria on 20 April 1889. Determined to become a great artist, he left home in Linz in 1907 to study in Vienna, although his application to the Academy of Fine Arts was rejected twice due to the poor quality of his work. Struggling to survive in Vienna, he worked as a labourer and sold paintings of city landmarks.

Hitler enrolled in the German Army during the First World War in 1914, reaching the rank of corporal. He received the Iron Cross First Class for bravery and was badly wounded in the leg as well as being temporarily blinded by mustard gas.

In 1919 he joined the German Workers' Party (DAP), forerunner to the National Socialist German Workers' Party (NSDAP), better known as the Nazi Party. He became leader of the Nazi Party in 1921, a highly passionate speaker able to inspire his audiences, denouncing communism and denigrating Jews as being at the heart of conspiracies against the German people. During his time in power, Hitler's views on German racial purity and his hatred for Jews would lead to the genocide of an estimated six million Jews and millions of other people considered to be racially or physically inferior.

Leading the Nazi Party into power, Hitler became Chancellor of Germany on 30 January 1933. He courted popularity by railing against the Treaty of Versailles, which had imposed reparations on Germany following the First World War; he galvanized German industry to accelerate economic recovery; he began to annex territories claimed as German; and he vastly expanded Germany's military capabilities.

In September 1939 Hitler sent German forces into Poland as part of his expansion programme, fully realizing that this would lead to war with Britain and France. The German Army swept aside all opposition and entered Paris on 14 June 1940, at which point Italian fascist dictator Benito Mussolini brought Italy into the war on Germany's side. Within months, what Hitler described as his Third Reich ("Third Empire") covered most of Europe and North Africa, yet by late 1941 the Soviet Union and the United States of America would join Britain to stand against Germany, spelling the beginning of the end, albeit that the war continued for four more years.

As the Red Army closed on Berlin in 1945, Hitler married his companion, Eva Braun, and within two days, on 30 April 1945, they had committed suicide rather than face capture.

On 17 May 1939 the king and queen arrived in Quebec, Canada, aboard the ocean liner *Empress of Australia*. They toured Canada from coast to coast, greeted by enthusiastic crowds wherever they went. The aim was to ensure that Canada would stand alongside Britain in any forthcoming conflict and the tour was seen as a great success. Accompanied by Prime Minister Mackenzie King of Canada, the royal couple travelled south to the USA, meeting President Roosevelt, visiting the 1939 New York World's Fair and the White House in Washington, DC, as well as the president's private residence at Hyde Park. It was the first time that a British monarch had ever been to the USA and, given that so many Americans had supported Edward VIII in his desire to marry Wallis Simpson, the welcome that the king and queen received from the general public was hugely positive. Their visit went a long way toward bolstering the ties between Britain and the USA.

The royal couple returned to Canada where the public's appetite for them had scarcely diminished. In St John's, Newfoundland and Labrador, the town's 50,000 population doubled as spectators flooded in from near and far. The king and queen sailed for home on 15 June and within 10 weeks of their return, on 3 September, George VI made a radio broadcast to the nation to declare that Britain was at war with Germany.

The princesses were at the royal family's summer retreat at Balmoral in Scotland when the announcement was made and, for a time, that was where they stayed. On their return to London, they were sent out of the capital to Windsor, along with Crawfie. The king and queen remained at Buckingham Palace, although they ultimately stayed in Windsor overnight, commuting back into the capital each morning. When bombs began to fall on London, the palace at first escaped any damage, but on 13 September 1940 the king and queen had a narrow escape when the palace was hit. There was significant damage and a number of workmen were wounded. One later died. The incident brought renewed calls from the government for the royal family, or at least the princesses, to be evacuated to Canada. The queen declared: "The children will not leave unless I do. I shall not leave unless their father does, and the king will not leave the country in any circumstances, whatever."

Winston Churchill: The Greatest Briton

Grandson of the Duke of Marlborough, Churchill was born at the ancestral home in Blenheim Palace in Oxfordshire, England, on 30 November 1874. His father, Lord Randolph Churchill, was a politician and his mother came from a wealthy American family.

Although intelligent and capable, at school Churchill was a poor student. He did apply himself enough to pass the entrance exam for Harrow School in 1888 and was later accepted (on his third attempt) into the Royal Military College (later Academy) Sandhurst. He graduated in 1895 and was commissioned as a second lieutenant in the 4th Hussars. Churchill served in India, Sudan and in the Second Boer War, also working as a war correspondent for various British newspapers. He continued to write articles and books throughout his life and would go on to win the Nobel Prize for Literature in 1953.

In 1900 Churchill entered politics. He was elected as the Conservative MP for Oldham in Lancashire, although he subsequently switched allegiance to the Liberal Party. He became Home Secretary and First Lord of the Admiralty but resigned from government amid widespread criticism of his handling of the disastrous Gallipoli operation. He rejoined the British Army, serving for a time with the Royal Scots Fusiliers on the Western Front.

By July 1917 Churchill was back in government under Lloyd George as Minister of Munitions and he held a variety of posts, including Chancellor of the Exchequer, up to 1929. For much of the 1930s he was out of favour politically, but when the Second World War began he was once more appointed First Lord of the Admiralty and when Neville Chamberlain resigned he became prime minister. Despite his inspirational leadership during the war years, Churchill was voted out of office in 1945. He was re-elected as prime minister six years later, serving until he retired in 1955. He was an MP until 1964 and died in 1965.

In a 2002 poll for a BBC TV series, the nation voted Sir Winston Leonard Spencer Churchill the greatest Briton who ever lived.

The royal family were determined to share the traumas of the British people and as the war intensified they became a symbol of courage and defiance that led Adolf Hitler to describe the queen as "the most dangerous woman in Europe".

CHAPTER THREE

WAR & PEACE

By the time that Winston Churchill became prime minister on 10 May 1940, the war was already going badly for the Allies. Within three weeks, the evacuation of troops from the beaches of Dunkirk would begin and in less than a month British forces in Norway would be withdrawn. Britain was to stand alone in Europe with the spectre of invasion looming over the English Channel.

So many troops and so much equipment had been lost in the retreat from Europe that the only units at full strength, ready to defend the English coast, were Canadian soldiers who had begun arriving in Britain just before Christmas 1939. Church bells were silenced, to be rung only as warning bells in the event of invasion. Roadside signposts were removed to hamper enemy troop movements; trenches and anti-tank ditches were dug; barbed wire and mines were laid on potential landing grounds; concrete gun emplacements were hastily built, not only on the coast but also along defensive lines inland; and Local Defence Volunteers, who came to be known as "Dad's Army", patrolled their neighbourhoods, scanned the skies for paratroops and prepared to defend their communities.

As if fear of invasion were not enough, Britain also faced up to the terror of the Luftwaffe (German air force) bombers. Because there were strong concerns that, as in the trenches during the First World War, poison gas might be used, the distribution of gas masks had begun as early as 1938. Family air raid shelters were erected in domestic gardens, communal shelters were created in public parks, and London Underground station platforms doubled as refuges when the bombers came over.

The first air raid alerts had come within hours of war being declared and the first German aircraft to probe Britain's defences began appearing within a week. Once the Luftwaffe was able to establish bases all along the Channel coast, all of the RAF's bases, all of Britain's industrial hinterland and every major British city was well within range of the bombers.

In the North Atlantic, German U-boats roamed at will, targeting Merchant Navy vessels bringing desperately needed food supplies to Britain. While planning the invasion, Hitler was prepared to bomb and starve Britain into submission, yet he was never able to crush the British spirit, and the British royal family, who had made themselves highly visible figureheads, personified that indomitable defiance.

A FAMILY AT WAR

King George VI and Queen Elizabeth were determined that they should be seen to be standing by the people of Britain during the war years. They toured hospitals, factories, dockyards, military bases and the ravaged streets of bomb-damaged homes in cities all over the country, especially London's East End – there, the docks and warehouses were the primary target but the homes of ordinary Londoners were also devastated. Enemy bombers had deliberately targeted Buckingham Palace several times and when the first bomb damage was sustained, the queen declared: "I am glad that we have been bombed. At least now I can look the East End in the face."

By the middle of September 1940, it became clear to the German High Command that it would not be able to destroy the RAF and achieve the air superiority over the south of England that was vital to its invasion plans. The immediate threat of invasion was over and daylight bombing raids ceased, although night bombing of British cities increased, just as RAF bombers, of course, pounded German cities, bases and industrial targets.

The queen continued to tour bomb sites and wrote to Queen Mary on 19 October describing one scene in Stoke Newington, London, where rescuers were, "digging people out from a block of flats which collapsed on top of them. They fear two hundred dead, owing to the fact that the water main burst and drowned many." She was devastated and exhausted by what she witnessed, but she never stopped going, although she confessed in a letter to her sister, Mary, that, "...I loathe going round these bombed places, I am a beastly coward and it breaks one's heart to see such misery and sadness. On the other hand, the spirit of the people is wonderful..." The queen was driven by a sense of duty, something that she was to pass on to her daughter.

The royal family was not insulated from the effects of the war. The damage to Buckingham Palace included having most of the windows blown out. They were boarded up, which made most of the palace gloomy, cold and draughty. The house in Bruton Street where Princess Elizabeth had been born was destroyed, as was the house at 145 Piccadilly. The king's brother, Prince Henry, was on active service with the British Army and was wounded when an enemy aircraft attacked his staff car. His other brother, Prince George, was killed in a plane crash in 1942 while serving with the RAF.

The king threw himself into working for the war effort. He had long weekly meetings with Prime Minister Winston Churchill to discuss every aspect of the war, usually with the queen in attendance, and as well as an endless list of official engagements at home, he visited troops in war zones whenever it could be arranged. He was in France with British forces in December 1939, in North Africa in 1943, in Normandy in 1944 just 10 days after the D-Day landings, in Italy in 1944 and in northern Europe in 1944. He even, after a great deal of badgering from Princess Elizabeth, allowed his eldest daughter to leave the relative safety of Windsor Castle and join the British Army.

THE PRINCESSES IN THE CASTLE

Princess Elizabeth and Princess Margaret spent much of the war at Windsor Castle, from where Princess Elizabeth, with Margaret's help and under the queen's supervision, made her first radio broadcast. She spoke to the children of the nation, Commonwealth and empire on the *Children's Hour* radio programme, telling children who had been evacuated to areas safe from the bombing of the cities and children of those absent on military service: "My sister Margaret Rose and I feel so much for you, for we too know from experience what it means to be away from those we love most of all."

Life for the royal family was not as it had been before the war. They shared many of the hardships faced by the rest of the country. When the USA's First Lady, Eleanor Roosevelt, came to visit the UK in 1942, she was shocked by the condition of Buckingham Palace, including the black lines painted on the bath to show how far it should be filled to avoid wasting fuel by heating too much water. Most food was rationed, although bread and potatoes were only rationed after the war. Mrs Roosevelt wrote in her daily newspaper column: "Everyone is urged to eat potatoes so potatoes usually appear in two forms at every meal. In the factory where we had lunch today there was a wonderful Lancashire pie, which ordinarily has layers of various meats with potatoes in between. Now they use mushrooms and any little scraps of meat they can obtain. In spite of which the pie is still good."

Mrs Roosevelt was visiting US service personnel, who had started arriving in Britain only weeks after the Japanese bombing of Pearl Harbor on 7 December 1941, which drew the USA into the war and spread the conflict throughout the Far East. Although the princesses were kept safe in Windsor, where the dungeons served as air raid shelters and there were delightful distractions, such as the crown jewels wrapped in newspaper and hidden in a cellar, the sisters were well aware of the progress of the war. Princess Elizabeth was in regular correspondence with Prince Philip of Greece, who served as an officer in the Royal Navy on postings to ships in the Far East as well as the Mediterranean and on convoy duties closer to home, so she had a very good idea of how enormous the conflict had become. By the time she was 16, and had publicly registered at a Labour Exchange for Wartime Youth Service, Princess Elizabeth was desperate to become more involved in the war effort. Her father made her Colonel of the Grenadier Guards and she inspected the regiment on her 16th birthday, but ceremonial duties were not exactly what she had in mind.

The king knew that he had to keep his daughter, the future monarch, safely out of danger during the war but he eventually allowed her to join the Auxiliary Territorial Service (ATS), where she was taught vehicle maintenance and learned to drive. She wore her ATS uniform when she appeared on the balcony at Buckingham Palace toward the end of the war on VE Day in May 1945 alongside her father, mother, sister and Winston Churchill, all waving to the huge crowds that had gathered at the palace gates. The princesses could see people celebrating, singing and dancing, and they persuaded their father to let them slip out of the palace to join in the revelry. He did, but he insisted that they went as part of a group, accompanied by some young Guards' officers. Princess Elizabeth later (as queen) recalled that they mingled with the crowd outside the palace: "We cheered the king and queen on the balcony and then walked miles through the street. I remember lines of unknown people linking arms and walking down Whitehall, all of us just swept along on a tide of happiness and relief."

One teenager from Harrow, who had travelled to London to join the celebrations, danced with Princess Elizabeth in Trafalgar Square. He told her that he recognized her and she asked him not to tell anyone else. He later told his family and friends all about it but no one believed him until the story of the princesses' VE Day adventure finally came out years later.

LOOKING TO THE FUTURE

The immediate postwar years in Britain were bleak times. Rationing was still in force, with goods only slowly being de-rationed. Meat was still rationed up to 1954. There was a housing shortage and a scarcity of

Clement Attlee: The Man who Defeated Churchill

On 5 July 1945 there was a General Election in the United Kingdom. Germany had surrendered in May, Japan was to follow suit in just two months, but heroic wartime leader Winston Churchill was defeated on the home front by Clement Attlee.

Clement Richard Attlee was born in Putney, southwest London, on 3 January 1883. One of eight children in a comfortably affluent family, he was educated at private schools before studying history at Oxford University, graduating in 1904. He trained as a barrister and worked in his father's law firm before undertaking voluntary work in London's East End, where he encountered dreadful poverty that inspired his devotion to socialism. In 1914 he enlisted in the army, despite initially being considered too old, and was commissioned as a captain, later promoted to major. He saw action at Gallipoli and in North Africa, where he was wounded, as well as in France.

Attlee returned to work at the London School of Economics, where he had lectured before the war, but quickly became involved in politics. In 1922 he married Violet Millar. The couple were to have four children and remained together until her death in 1964. He was also elected as the Labour MP for Limehouse in 1922, rising steadily through the Labour Party ranks to become its leader in 1935. He was deputy prime minister in Churchill's wartime coalition government but campaigned for Labour when the coalition was dissolved in 1945.

The result was a landslide victory for Attlee, with voters desperate for the Labour Party's proposed reforms. Attlee fulfilled his pledges of full employment, the nationalization of public utilities and the Bank of England, and the creation of the National Health Service. Welfare reforms included child benefit and funeral benefit; married women were allowed to work in the civil service; there were pensions for firefighters; better wages for police officers; and better conditions of employment for miners. The changes were immense, but improvements in the lives of most people during the austere postwar years were slow in coming.

Attlee led Labour to a narrow victory in the 1950 General Election, but was subsequently defeated in 1951 by Churchill's Conservatives. He continued as Labour leader, retiring in 1955 when he was created Earl Attlee and Viscount Prestwood. He died on 8 October 1967, aged 84.

labour with five million men and women serving in the British armed forces in 1945. Some would not be released back into civilian life until well into 1947.

Yet there were also things to look forward to. In 1946 it was announced that the Olympic Games would be held in London in 1948. These became known as the "Austerity Games". No new sports venues were built and the athletes from 59 countries (Germany and Japan were not invited) who attended were housed in military barracks or university accommodation. They were also offered extra rations to maintain their fitness levels. The Games were a huge success.

In 1947 plans were unveiled for the Festival of Britain in 1951. Originally conceived to celebrate the centenary of the Great Exhibition of 1851, the festival grew into a nationwide event showcasing British science, technology, industrial design, architecture and the arts. Although centred on the South Bank in London, there were to be touring events and permanent exhibitions all over the country.

And then there were rumours of a royal wedding. Princess Elizabeth was 13 years old when she, along with Princess Margaret and their parents, paid a visit to Britannia Royal Naval College at Dartmouth aboard the royal yacht HMY *Victoria and Albert*. One of the officer cadets, Prince Philip of Greece, was detailed to escort the princesses during their visit. Philip was the nephew of Lord Louis Mountbatten, who was the king's cousin. When the visit was over, *Victoria and Albert* departed, with a fleet of small boats as her escort. The boats were manned by cadets and all turned for home after a time, except for the one with Philip at the helm. He was ordered back by loudhailer but the handsome 18-year-old had made a serious impression on the young Princess Elizabeth.

In a 1947 letter to Betty Shew, an author writing about the royal wedding, Princess Elizabeth described how when Philip was on leave he "spent various weekends away with us at Windsor" and that they started seeing more of each other when he was given a shore posting at the Royal Navy's Petty Officer School in Wiltshire: "He'd spend weekends with us and when the school was closed he spent six weeks at Balmoral."

Prince Philip recalled spending time with the royal family but played down any romantic interest between him and Princess Elizabeth in the

Mao Zedong: Chairman of Terror

Mao Zedong was born on 26 December 1893, the son of a wealthy farmer. He was well educated and an avid reader, writing poetry and studying political theory during his teenage years. During the Xinhai Revolution of 1911, Mao joined the revolutionary army that overthrew the last Emperor of China to establish the Republic of China.

While working at Beijing University Mao studied Marxist-Leninist theories and helped to form the Communist Party of China (CPC) in 1921. Six years later the CPC, led by Mao, began a revolutionary war against the ruling Kuomintang (KMT) party. After 10 years, the two sides joined forces to fight the Japanese, a war that would last until 1945. The Chinese coalition had help from both the Soviet Union and the USA but with the Japanese defeat at the end of the Second World War, the Chinese Civil War resumed. The Soviets backed Mao's CPC and the Americans the KMT.

Mao vanquished the KMT and established the People's Republic of China in 1949. By now widely known as Chairman Mao, he instigated wide-ranging reforms, purging all opposition, creating collective farms and beginning a programme of industrialization. He also supported Kim Il-Sung during the Korean War, sending in Chinese troops when Kim's forces were pushed back almost to the Chinese border. At home, Mao's reforms – along with new, state-imposed farming techniques and a series of droughts – resulted in famine and the deaths of an estimated 45 million Chinese between 1958 and 1962. In 1966 Mao launched the Cultural Revolution, repressing any opposition to the CPC's totalitarian regime, destroying historical artefacts and religious buildings and subjecting millions to imprisonment, torture, hard labour and execution.

Mao was married four times. His first was an arranged marriage to Lou Yixiu, organized by their respective fathers when Mao was 14 and Lou 18. Mao refused to recognize Lou as his wife and she died of dysentery in 1910. Mao married Yang Kaihu in 1920 and they had three children. Yang was executed by the KMT in 1930. Mao's third wife was He Zizhen, whom he married while Yang was still alive. They had six children, but while she was in the Soviet Union having a battle wound treated in 1938, Mao married his fourth wife, actress Jiang Qing, with whom he had one child. Mao stayed with Jiang until his death in 1976.

early days, saying, "I knew half the people here, they were all relations. It isn't so extraordinary to be on kind of family relationship terms."

Nevertheless, a romance did flourish and the prince proposed to the princess at Balmoral in September 1946. She accepted, but there was to be no public announcement. The king was concerned that his daughter was too young at only 20 years old and urged that any announcement be delayed until after the forthcoming tour to South Africa in February 1947. The king, the queen and their daughters were to be gone for four months, and during that time Princess Elizabeth would celebrate her 21st birthday. In a speech broadcast on radio and filmed for posterity, she welcomed "the opportunity to speak to all the peoples of the British Commonwealth and Empire" and said, "I declare before you all that my whole life, whether it be long or short, shall be devoted to your service and the service of our great imperial family to which we all belong." Nothing could better illustrate the notion of duty instilled in her by her mother and father.

While the royal family was away, Prince Philip began making preparations for the marriage announcement. He was Prince Philip of Greece and Denmark, part of the Danish house of Schleswig-Holstein-Sonderburg-Glücksburg. Having changed their name to Windsor to shake off their German ties (Schleswig-Holstein was an area long disputed by the Danes and the Germans), this was not the time to reintroduce them. Prince Philip renounced all claims to his Greek and Danish titles and changed his name to Mountbatten. He was now Lieutenant Philip Mountbatten of His Majesty's Royal Navy, but he also had to put the wheels in motion to become a naturalized British subject.

When the engagement was announced in July 1947, the young couple made the first of their many appearances together on the balcony at Buckingham Palace, waving to the thousands of well-wishers who had gathered at the palace gates. Immediately prior to their wedding on 20 November 1947, King George VI bestowed on Philip the style of His Royal Highness and made him Duke of Edinburgh, Earl of Merioneth and Baron Greenwich.

They were married in a glittering ceremony at Westminster Abbey, which was recorded for radio and broadcast to an estimated 200 million

Kim Il-Sung: The Eternal President

The man who established a ruling dynasty in the Democratic People's Republic of Korea (DPRK), known as North Korea, was born on 15 April 1912 and originally named Kim Song-Ju. When he was an infant his family fled across the border into Manchuria to escape the Japanese occupation of Korea.

At school in China, Kim became intrigued by communism and by 1931 he was a member of Mao Zedong's Communist Party of China. He became involved with anti-Japanese guerrilla groups, rising through the ranks until, in 1935, he changed his name to Kim Il-Sung, meaning "Kim of the sun", and the troops led by him were nicknamed "Kim Il-Sung's Division". In 1937 they captured a Japanese-held town on the Korean border. Kim was later to train in the USSR and became an officer in the Soviet Red Army.

In August 1945 the Soviets occupied the northern part of Korea and by December Stalin had installed Kim as the local Communist Party leader. Kim became leader of the DPRK when it was established in 1948. Kim formed the Korean People's Army by recruiting guerrillas who had fought the Japanese and his military forces were equipped by the Soviet Union, with Stalin ultimately agreeing to Kim's invasion of South Korea (Republic of Korea or ROK) on 25 June 1950 in a bid to reunify the country under his rule. United Nations forces, led by the USA, defended South Korea and Kim was forced to agree an armistice on 27 July 1953.

Kim's ruthless suppression of any domestic opposition, his prison camps, the abuses of human rights and summary executions in North Korea gave the United Nations huge cause for concern, not least because his forces continued to involve themselves in border skirmishes. When North Korean naval vessels captured a US Navy surveillance ship in international waters in 1968, taking 83 prisoners (one of whom was killed), it caused an international incident, heightening Cold War tensions.

Although he died in 1994, his state-sponsored cult endures. His portrait is displayed throughout the country and his birthday is "The Day of the Sun" public holiday. He was given the posthumous title "Eternal President of the Republic" and his preserved body is on display behind glass in the Kumsusan Palace of the Sun in Pyongyang. Before he died, Kim ensured that his oldest son, Kim Jong-Il, would succeed him as North Korea's leader.

people around the world. There were 2,000 wedding guests, although none of the Duke of Edinburgh's German relations (his sisters had married German princes) were invited. Once again, crowds thronged London's streets to catch a glimpse of the happy couple, and in such austere times – when extra clothing ration coupons had to be found for the material to make the princess's wedding dress – the spectacle of a royal occasion brought an element of cheer to the nation.

The duke and duchess moved into Clarence House in London, just a short stroll down The Mall from Buckingham Palace, and their first child, Prince Charles, was born within a year on 14 November 1948. There was growing optimism toward the end of the 1940s with people beginning to look ahead and plan for the future, but by the time that Prince Charles's sister, Princess Anne, was born on 15 August 1950 Britain was at war once more.

CHAPTER FOUR

THE YOUNG

QUEEN

By the beginning of the 1950s, Britain was a country most definitely looking to the future. The Labour government's introduction of the National Health Service in 1946 was proving to be a huge success and industry was booming, with Britain's shipyards the busiest in the world. Britain exported more coal, textiles, steel and cars than any other country in Europe and in 1952 the all-British de Havilland Comet – the world's first jet airliner – went into service.

There were new clothes with the "New Look" fashions that had been introduced in the late 1940s, which allowed women to luxuriate in dresses with full skirts and the sort of detailing that had been banned to save cloth during the war years. Food was becoming more plentiful, although certain items were rationed well into the 1950s, and the wartime practice of "grow your own" in gardens and allotments was still officially encouraged.

The Second World War, in fact, was never far away. There were constant reminders in the rubble-strewn waste ground that had once been homes and factories or the bomb-damaged buildings that still stood unrepaired due to a shortage of materials and manpower. Immigrant workers had begun to arrive to boost the workforce, with the first influx from Jamaica in 1948, but there were fewer than 140,000 black or Asian people in the country in 1951 and of the 50 million population only around 3 per cent had not been born in Britain.

War was also still very much a reality for Britain's young men. Between the ages of 17 and 21, they were required to do National Service in the armed forces for two years. National Service was not compulsory for women. National Servicemen fought alongside regular enlisted personnel in the Korean War (1950–53), against communist guerrillas in the jungles of Malaya (1948–60), against terrorists in Cyprus (1955–60), during the Mau Mau Uprising in Kenya (1952–64) and in the Suez invasion in 1956. Their grandfathers had fought in the First World War, their fathers had fought in the Second World War and they, too, were expected to join the military, with Britain's armed forces around four times the size that they are today.

The commander-in-chief of the British armed forces is, of course, the monarch, and the king, who had led the nation through the war years so heroically, tragically passed away in 1952, leaving Britain with a new, young queen. Some wondered whether this slight, delicate-looking mother-of-two would be up to the job.

THE DEATH OF THE KING

King George VI passed away peacefully in his sleep at Sandringham on 6 February 1952. In a radio broadcast the following day, Prime Minister Winston Churchill recited his eulogy to the king, acknowledging that George VI had struggled through the previous few months knowing that he had not long to live. He said:

> During these last months the King talked with death as if death were a companion and acquaintance whom he recognised and did not fear. In the end, death came as a friend, and after a happy day of sunshine and sport, after a "goodnight" to those who loved him

best, he fell asleep as every man or woman who strives to fear God and nothing else in the world may hope to do.

The king's wife, Queen Elizabeth, who would now take the official title Queen Elizabeth The Queen Mother (thus avoiding any confusion with her daughter who was now Queen Elizabeth II) privately blamed her brother-in-law, the Duke of Windsor, and Wallis Simpson for the decline in her husband's health. She firmly believed that had the duke, when still King Edward VIII, put his duty to the Crown before his personal contentment, as she and her husband had been obliged to do, George would have avoided the hideously stressful ordeals through which he had battled. He would have lived longer.

The strain of leading the country, especially through six long years of war, had certainly taken a toll on the king's health, but so too had his smoking habit. Like his father and grandfather before him, George VI was a heavy smoker, and it was undoubtedly a major factor in the ailments that plagued him. He was diagnosed with arteriosclerosis and Buerger's disease, both of which involve a narrowing of blood vessels due to build-ups of fatty deposits and are closely associated with smoking. The consequent restriction of blood flow caused George VI such pain in his legs that he resorted to repeatedly kicking his desk or doorposts to try to keep his circulation going. In March 1949 he underwent an operation to relieve a blockage in the arteries of his right leg. The operation was a success but, had it not been, his surgeons may have had to amputate the limb.

Then, in September 1951, having been diagnosed with cancer, George VI had his left lung removed. An operating theatre was set up in Buckingham Palace because this was felt to be the best way to minimize stress levels for the king and also to keep the serious nature of the operation as discreet as possible. Nevertheless, the fact that the king was undergoing surgery made the front pages of the newspapers and crowds gathered outside the palace gates, where bulletins were posted on the railings.

It became clear during the operation that the cancer in the left lung was also present in the right. This was not made public. Only his surgeons and Winston Churchill knew the truth – from then on the king was living on borrowed time.

Charles de Gaulle: Saviour of France

A graduate of Saint-Cyr, France's military academy, Charles André Joseph Marie de Gaulle was an officer in the French Army during the First World War. He was involved in heavy fighting, on different occasions being shot in the knee, shot in the hand and bayoneted in the leg. Following the bayonet incident at Verdun, he was knocked out by a shell and captured, spending 32 months as a prisoner of war.

Born on 22 November 1890, de Gaulle was the son of a college professor and as a child he was a voracious reader, concentrating mainly on history and philosophy. Had he not trained as an army officer he might well have become a historian. Following his service in the First World War, de Gaulle enjoyed a controversial military career, frequently at odds with his superiors about modern military tactics. By the time the Second World War broke out, he was in command of the French Fifth Army's light tanks. After the fall of France, he refused to capitulate and led the Free French forces in Britain, making radio broadcasts from London that called on the French people not to accept the German occupation or the German-controlled French government that had been installed in Vichy.

Following the Allied liberation of France in 1944, de Gaulle became head of the Provisional Government of the French Republic. Frustrated by political infighting, he resigned in 1946, although he remained actively involved in politics. By 1958, when various factions, including military leaders, seemed to be on the verge of plunging France into a civil war, de Gaulle was called upon to unite the country. He became prime minister and, a year later, President of France. He remained president until he resigned in 1969.

Although he presided over the decline of France as a colonial power, de Gaulle was insistent that the country should play a major, independent role on the world stage. He took France out of NATO and by 1960 the French had developed their own nuclear weapons, making France (at that time) the fourth nuclear power along with the USA, USSR and UK.

De Gaulle married Yvonne in 1921 and the couple had three children, Philippe, Elisabeth and Anne. He died suddenly of a ruptured blood vessel while relaxing at home in Colombey-les-Deux-Églises on 9 November 1970, just two weeks before his 80th birthday.

On 31 January 1952, Princess Elizabeth and the Duke of Edinburgh took off from London Airport on an official tour to Kenya, Ceylon (now Sri Lanka), Australia and New Zealand. The king and queen were to have made the trip but the king was not strong enough to travel. The king and queen were, however, at the airport with Princess Margaret to wave the couple goodbye. They then travelled to Sandringham and the king enjoyed a day's shooting on 5 February, the "sunshine and sport" referred to by Winston Churchill. He died of a heart attack during the night and was found in bed by his valet in the morning.

The king's coffin lay in St Mary Magdelene Church in Sandringham from 9 to 11 February before it was taken by train to King's Cross Station in London and on to Westminster Hall. There it was to remain until 15 February when London's streets were once more lined with mourners, standing silent and still as the watery winter sun struggled to penetrate a shroud of fog. The king's coffin, mounted on a gun carriage, was escorted in an elaborate procession through Parliament Square and down Whitehall, past the Cenotaph on the first stage of its journey to Windsor. The coffin was followed by a carriage in which rode the Queen, the Queen Mother, Princess Margaret and the king's sister, Princess Mary. Behind the carriage walked the four royal dukes: the Duke of Edinburgh, the Duke of Gloucester, the Duke of Kent and the Duke of Windsor. The king's brother had been invited to the funeral, Wallis Simpson had not.

The funeral took place in St George's Chapel, Windsor Castle, where the king was laid to rest in the Royal Vault, although his body was later transferred to the King George VI Memorial Chapel on its completion in 1969. There were many floral tributes at the funeral and on the card with the government's wreath Winston Churchill had written "For Valour", the two words that appear on the Victoria Cross.

THE GREAT SMOG

The light fog that had hung over George VI's funeral procession had become an ever more common feature of life in London by the 1950s. In winter, atmospheric conditions could produce what became known as "smog" – a toxic combination of smoke and fog. People had come to accept smog as part of everyday life in the city, but in early December 1952 what became known as the "Great Smog" brought the city to a standstill and resulted in the deaths of so many Londoners that it was clear that things had to change.

In many ways, smog was the price that Britain paid for its industrial success. The Industrial Revolution had been powered by coal – and so much coal was burned in the capital that when there was no breeze and a blanket of fog descended over the city the moist air turned into a deadly chemical soup.

Coal was used everywhere in Britain. At one time it was used in factories to provide steam power and almost every home in the land was heated with open fires burning coal, as were most offices. At the beginning of the twentieth century over one-quarter of Britain's workforce was employed in the coal industry. By the 1950s there were 19,000 steam trains on the country's rail network, and a train running from London to Newcastle would burn six tons of coal. A constant stream of trains, belching smoke into the atmosphere, brought commuters from the suburbs into the capital every morning and took them home again at night, yet London's biggest polluters were not the trains but the coal-fired power stations.

Battersea Power Station's four iconic chimneys were the worst culprits. This one power station consumed a million tons of coal a year and contrived with others on the banks of the Thames to deliver smoke, soot and gases into the air which, when blended with the water in a foggy atmosphere, left hundreds of tons of sulphur dioxide as well as hydrochloric acid and sulphuric acid lingering in the air breathed by Londoners.

On the morning of 5 December 1952, the sky above the capital was a clear, bright blue. London had been gripped by cold weather for weeks, and fires in homes and offices were stoked to ward off the chill. During the day a haze of fog drifted in over the city and a temperature inversion – a high layer of warmer air that trapped colder air beneath it – hovered over the whole area. Day after day, fog and smoke mixed to form the thickest smog, reeking of sulphur, that London had ever seen. Londoners were advised to stay at home and to cover their mouths with handkerchiefs or scarves to filter the foul air, but even indoors grimy, sooty deposits accumulated on window ledges, shelves, sinks and kitchen work surfaces.

Out in the street, policemen on point duty wore masks, but not only was the air quality atrocious, the smog also blocked out the sunlight and turned day into night. Vehicle headlights were almost superfluous, bus conductors walked ahead of buses carrying lamps, drivers abandoned their cars, boats on the river were forced to tie up – no one could see where they were going. Flights from London Airport were grounded, trains were cancelled and buses were recalled to their depots. Apart from the London Underground trains, the capital was at a standstill.

During the weekend of 6 and 7 December, football matches were cancelled because spectators would not have been able to see the pitches – if they had managed to reach the venues. Even some cinemas cancelled movie screenings because the smog inside the buildings made it too difficult for the audience to see the screen.

Worst of all was the horrendous effect that the smog had on people's health. All of London's hospitals were inundated with patients suffering from breathing difficulties. The smog was killing people. When the figures were analysed, the number of deaths in London in the week leading up to 13 December were shown to be more than twice that of the same week the previous year. Almost 6,000 people died in December 1952 and in subsequent years the long-term effects of the smog are thought to have been responsible for the premature deaths of more than twice that number.

The shock of the Great Smog brought about legislation to limit emissions, with the Clean Air Act of 1956 introducing changes that would begin to guarantee Londoners air that was fit to breathe.

THE DAWN OF THE NEW ELIZABETHAN ERA

The swirl of the Great Smog was still some way off in the future when the devastating news about the death of George VI broke. Ironically, the person to whom the death of the king meant most was in danger of being one of the last to hear about it. Princess Elizabeth and the Duke of Edinburgh had been in Kenya for six days and were due to travel on to Ceylon. They had been at the Treetops Hotel, a sprawling timber lodge built in the branches of a giant fig tree in the Aberdare National Park, taking a break from official engagements. They were watching elephants, rhino and giraffes when the king died and the princess, although she knew nothing of it at the time, had become a queen.

With no instant communication possible, informing the Queen that her father had died would not have been easy while she was at Treetops and the difficulty was compounded by the fact that when the message "Hyde Park Corner" – the code that meant the king had died – was transmitted to Government House in Nairobi early in the morning of 6 February, the High Commissioner was already en route to Mombasa, almost 300 miles (over 480 kilometres) away. The royal couple were due to set sail from Mombasa for Ceylon. Without the High Commissioner, no one could find the keys to the safe where the codebook was kept.

The new queen and the Duke of Edinburgh, still unaware of the king's death, travelled to Sagana Lodge, a country house that had been given to them as a wedding present by the Kenyan people, on the first stage of their journey to Mombasa. There the duke's private secretary, Michael Parker, took a phone call with the dreadful news. He immediately informed the duke, whom he said, "looked as if you'd dropped half the world on him". The duke then informed his wife that her father had died.

The Queen and the Duke of Edinburgh were rushed to an airstrip at Nanyuki to take the quickest route home. They were flown to Entebbe in Uganda, where a longer-range aircraft waited to take them on a 2,260-mile (3,360-kilometre) flight, crossing the Sahara, to RAF El Adem in Libya. There the aircraft was refuelled. Having left Entebbe at 9 p.m. on 6 February, they arrived at London Airport 19 hours later, on the evening of 7 February. The prime minister and other dignitaries stood patiently on the runway while suitable black attire was brought for the Queen to change into. The black funeral outfit that had accompanied her on tour in case it should be required when she was abroad had been packed and sent ahead to Mombasa with the rest of her clothes. There had been no time to retrieve her baggage, so a different black coat, hat and gloves were waiting for her at London Airport. With newsreel cameras and press photographers waiting for the first photographs of Queen Elizabeth II, she needed to be seen to be in mourning.

The following day the Queen met with her Accession Council where she gave a speech to her Privy Councillors, who included leading politicians and civil servants not only from Britain but also from the whole Commonwealth, saying, "I pray that God will help me to discharge worthily this heavy task that has been laid upon me so early in my life."

There are a number of photographs of the young Princess Elizabeth standing at her father's shoulder as he sits at his desk, explaining to her something of the everyday duties of the monarch, yet Queen Elizabeth II had not had as much time to prepare for the role as she had expected. She later said, "In a way I didn't have an apprenticeship because my father died much too young."

The Queen had no choice but to pick up the reins and continue the work of the monarch. She and the Duke of Edinburgh had spent many months turning Clarence House into their London home, but, just as she had been obliged as a young girl to move into Buckingham Palace with her parents, now she was obliged as a young woman to move in once again because Buckingham Palace was, and remains, the official residence of the monarch.

Planning for her coronation began straight away and the Queen insisted that the Duke of Edinburgh take a major role in organizing the ceremony. He was the person she could most trust to keep her informed every step of the way to ensure that the ceremony threw up no surprises. In the meantime, the Queen had to keep pace with day-to-day business. She later described coming to terms with her role: "It was a question of maturing into something that you got used to doing and accepting that it was your fate. It's a job for life. Most people have a job and then they go home and in this existence, the job and the life go on together."

The coronation date was set for 2 June 1953 and the Queen began to prepare herself by studying photographs, film footage and recordings of her father's coronation. She had, of course, been present at the event, but she wanted to familiarize herself with every detail. Whenever she had time, she practised getting in and out of the state coach, using

Dwight D. Eisenhower: The Soldier Statesman

Eisenhower's family was originally named Eisenhauer (meaning "iron miner") and they emigrated from Karlsbrunn, a German village near the French border, to Pennsylvania, around 1741. By the time that Eisenhower's father, David, was born in 1863, the name had been Anglicized to Eisenhower. David married Ida and they had seven sons. When their third boy, David Dwight, was born on 14 October 1890, the family was living in Denison, Texas. David Dwight's mother eventually reversed his names to avoid confusion with his father. All of the boys had the nickname "Ike", a name that stuck with Dwight.

In 1911 Dwight was accepted into the United States Military Academy, West Point, graduating in 1915. When the USA became involved in the First World War in 1917, Dwight requested active service but was instead promoted to captain and sent to Pennsylvania to train the new Tank Corps. He rose steadily through the ranks, becoming a brigadier general in 1941. When the USA entered the Second World War, Eisenhower had no battle experience, yet he was to command the largest Allied operations of the war, including the D-Day landings in France. Hugely popular with his troops, he was referred to as "Ike".

After the war Eisenhower became the first Supreme Commander of the North Atlantic Treaty Organization (NATO), and in 1952 he ran for election as President of the United States. He won the election by a landslide and won again in 1956. His economic policies brought prosperity, he extended social security and signed the 1957 Civil Rights Act, helping to end racial segregation in the USA. He might have won a third term but was the first president to be limited to two terms by a 1951 amendment to the Constitution.

Eisenhower stood up to the USSR, China and communist expansion during the Cold War. He ensured that the USA led the United Nations during the Korean War and supported the new state of South Vietnam, but would not support the British and French invasion of Egypt during the Suez Crisis in 1956, forcing them to back down. When the Soviets launched their *Sputnik 1* satellite in 1957, Eisenhower oversaw the creation of NASA, ensuring the USA's place in outer space.

Although he ceased to be president in 1961, Eisenhower continued to be involved in politics for the rest of his life. He died on 28 March 1969. Married once, to Mamie Doud in 1916, the couple had two sons.

arrangements of chairs to represent the coach itself. She practised walking, trailing sheets behind her to represent the long train that she would wear on the day. Most of all, she practised walking straight-backed, at a sedate, solemn pace, wearing the crown. The crown is solid gold, a foot (30 centimetres) tall and weighs more than 5 pounds (over 2.2 kilograms). The Queen is a slight figure at just under 5 feet 4 inches (161.9 centimetres) and wearing the crown required a great deal of stamina.

Having borrowed the crown to practise with it, legend has it that she was able to wear it once when she visited her grandmother so that Queen Mary could see it on her granddaughter's head. Queen Mary's health was failing and it seemed unlikely that she would be well enough to attend the coronation. She insisted that should she die shortly before the coronation there should be no official period of mourning – nothing that would postpone her granddaughter's big day. Queen Mary died on 24 March 1953.

It might have been thought that the coronation of Queen Elizabeth II, coming as it did when the last elements of wartime rationing were still in place, should be scaled down, with less of the expensive pageantry than in previous coronations to suit these more austere times. Instead, the government decided that the coronation was to be an uplifting, glittering experience that would outshine any royal occasion to date. It would boost the nation's morale and show that Britain was confident, vibrant and looking to the future.

The day of the coronation began chilly and wet, although nothing could dampen the spirits of those who had come to see the coronation procession. Well-wishers had travelled from all over the country, some camping out on the pavement to ensure a good vantage point. Around 40,000 are believed to have come from the USA and berths on transatlantic liners were fully booked. It is estimated that there were two million crowding the streets that day. Lining the route were 15,000 troops who had been brought into the capital for the big occasion – the royal parks were full of tents to accommodate them. Marching in the procession in front of and following the state coach were 29,000 service personnel from throughout the Commonwealth, creating a dazzling display of pageantry that stretched for two miles (3.2 kilometres). The entire procession took around 45 minutes to pass any single point on the five-mile (eight-kilometre) route and the crowds were treated to a lingering view of the ornate state coach which, due to its great weight, can not exceed walking pace.

For those who could not make it into the capital, a new innovation allowed them to watch the procession and the ceremony live because BBC TV cameras had been allowed into Westminster Abbey. The Queen, deeply religious and sensitive in relation to the most sacred parts of the coronation ritual, had insisted that some elements of the ceremony, such as the anointing of the top of her chest with holy oil, should be excluded from being filmed, but most of the seven-hour proceedings were broadcast on television and radio, as well as being filmed in colour for subsequent cinema screenings. Sales of television sets in Britain rocketed in the build-up to the coronation and more than 20 million viewers tuned in, although there were only around 2.7 million television sets in the country. Families and neighbours watched together. Because international live broadcasts were not possible at that time, to give viewers in Canada and the USA the chance to watch the coronation, RAF jets flew the BBC footage across the Atlantic.

The Queen arrived at Westminster Abbey at 11 a.m. and inside there were 8,000 invited guests, including members of the British royal family and the nobility, Members of Parliament, foreign royalty, heads of state from the Commonwealth countries and dignitaries from all over the world. The first of all of them to pledge allegiance to the newly crowned Queen toward the end of the ceremony was her husband, the Duke of Edinburgh.

The coronation was a stunning spectacle and when the procession finally returned to Buckingham Palace, a mass of people that stretched from the palace gates all the way up The Mall cheered and roared for the Queen to appear on the balcony. Queen Elizabeth II did not disappoint, appearing with her husband, her family, her maids of honour and as many of the coronation party as could squeeze onto the balcony. The crowd called for her again and again, refusing to disperse despite the persistent rain, and she made her final appearance at midnight.

Fidel Castro: Freedom Fighter

If you were to choose the person who sent the greatest shock waves through the USA during the Cold War it would have to be Fidel Castro, the man who brought Soviet-style communism right into America's backyard.

Born Fidel Alejandro Castro Ruz on 13 August 1926, Castro was the son of an affluent farmer and was well educated, mainly at private schools. He studied law at the University of Havana from 1945 and it was there he became involved in politics, publicly denouncing government corruption.

He joined the mainly socialist Party of the Cuban People in 1947. Their anti-government protests were brutally suppressed and in 1948 Castro also took part in El Bogotazo, the violent anti-government riots in Colombia. In 1952 he stood for election to the House of Representatives but General Fulgencio Batista seized power in a military coup before the elections were held. Castro formed an underground movement to oppose the new right-wing regime, leading an armed uprising in 1953. Many of his followers were captured and executed. Castro was imprisoned but released under an amnesty in 1955. He travelled to Mexico with his brother, Raúl, and their supporters where they planned a revolution against Batista.

On his return to Cuba in December 1957, Castro began a guerrilla war that succeeded in deposing Batista in 1959. As prime minister, Castro nationalized industries owned by US companies and created a communist state. President Eisenhower authorized CIA support for a counter-revolution in Cuba, which resulted in the failed Bay of Pigs invasion in 1961, by which time President John F. Kennedy was in the White House.

When Castro's Soviet allies based nuclear missiles on the island in 1962, posing a direct threat to the USA, the Cuban Missile Crisis erupted. Kennedy demanded their removal and deployed a US Navy blockade to prevent further missile deliveries. Tension mounted, threatening war between the superpowers, until the Soviets agreed to withdraw provided that US missiles in Turkey were also removed.

Castro continued to involve Cuba in international affairs, sending troops to fight alongside revolutionary groups in countries such as Angola in 1975 and supporting budding socialist governments in Chile in 1970 as well as Grenada and Nicaragua in 1979. He became the President of Cuba in 1976, and in 2006 he ceded power to the vice president – his brother Raúl, who was elected president in 2008.

Married twice, to Mirta Díaz-Balart in 1948 (divorced in 1955) and Dalia Soto del Valle in 1980, Castro had at least nine children. He died on 25 November 2016.

Queen Victoria with her grandchildren Princess Victoria of York, Prince Edward (later Edward VIII), Prince Albert (later George VI) and baby Prince Henry in 1900.

Prince Henry, Duke of Gloucester; Edward, Prince of Wales (later Edward VIII); and Prince Albert, Duke of York (later George VI).

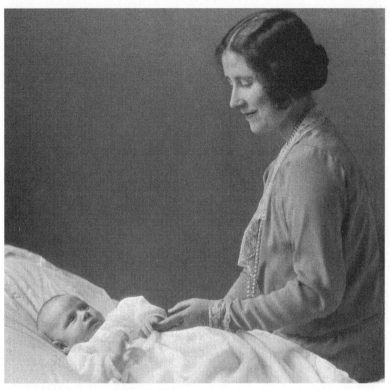

The king and queen's second child, Princess Margaret Rose, was born on 21 August 1930.

When the king finally allowed Princess Elizabeth to join the armed forces, she learned to drive, maintain and repair cars and trucks with the Auxiliary Territorial Service.

Princess Elizabeth and her husband, now Duke of Edinburgh, on the balcony
at Buckingham Palace on their wedding day, 20 November 1947.

The Queen and the Duke of Edinburgh inspecting Brownies
following a tree-planting ceremony in Gibraltar in 1954.

Prince Charles and Lady Diana Spencer at Buckingham Palace on the announcement of their engagement, 24 February 1981.

The Buckingham Palace "balcony kiss" has become an expected part of any royal wedding day.

Prince Harry and American actress Meghan Markle
announced their engagement on 27 November 2017.

The royal family aboard the Royal Barge Spirit of Chartwell,
watching the Thames Jubilee River Pageant go by.

CHAPTER FIVE

PARLIAMENT

& POLITICS

The second Christmas Day radio broadcast by Queen Elizabeth II was made not from the comfort of the family retreat at Sandringham, but from Government House in Auckland, New Zealand. Only a few months after her coronation in June 1953, the Queen and the Duke of Edinburgh embarked on a mammoth tour of the Commonwealth – a visit from the Queen being seen as the best way to promote unity and friendship between the Commonwealth nations and to preserve the unique global alliance at a time when monarchs and colonialism were being usurped by new political regimes the world over.

The implementation of apartheid race laws in South Africa, which was still part of the Commonwealth with Elizabeth as its queen, was causing increasing civil unrest.

Jordan, having become an independent kingdom in 1946 and no longer a British "Protectorate", under British jurisdiction, was still reeling from the assassination of King Abdullah in 1951. Abdullah's son, Talal, had become king but mental health problems had led to his enforced abdication in August 1952, making his son, Crown Prince Hussein, Jordan's third king in 13 months.

Pakistan, created in 1947 by the Partition of India, was a Dominion of which Elizabeth was monarch (at least until it became a republic in 1956) and the country's first prime minister, Liaqat Ali Khan, had fallen to an assassin's bullet in 1951.

The Commonwealth tour, taking in Australia and New Zealand, which the royal couple would have visited on the trip that was aborted due to the death of King George VI, was a way of maintaining Britain's influence and of keeping stability in an increasingly unstable world.

THE COMMONWEALTH TOUR OF 1953-54

The tour took the Queen and the duke away from their children for almost six months, from 25 November 1953 to 15 May 1954. It was a journey that was originally intended to be undertaken by her father, and a cargo liner, SS *Gothic*, had been refitted and painted white to become a "royal yacht" specifically for this cruise. The royal couple joined the *Gothic* in Jamaica, having flown in from Bermuda, the first stop on their tour. Then it was on to Panama and through the Panama Canal to visit Fiji and Tonga before arriving in New Zealand on 23 December.

During her Christmas broadcast, the Queen was at pains to present the Commonwealth as a modern institution that had a great deal to offer, with the monarchy serving to bind its members together:

Some people have expressed the hope that my reign may mark a new Elizabethan age. Frankly I do not myself feel at all like my great Tudor forebear, who was blessed with neither husband nor children, who ruled as a despot and was never able to leave her native shores.

...the Commonwealth bears no resemblance to the Empires of the past. It is an entirely new conception, built on the highest qualities of the spirit of man: friendship, loyalty and the desire for freedom and peace. To that new conception of an equal partnership of nations and races I shall give myself heart and soul every day of my life.

There was real concern that political activists in the Commonwealth territories, agitating for swift and complete independence from the UK, were gaining ground and the broadcast, like the tour, was intended to pour oil on troubled waters and have a calming effect. In Egypt, after all, where British troops had been stationed since the latter part of the nineteenth century, the monarchy had been overthrown in a coup organized by army officers led by Colonel Gamal Nasser. Britain had long-supported the regime in Egypt, with Sudan being jointly administered by the Egyptian and British governments. In 1898, as a young lieutenant in the Queen's 4th Hussars, Winston Churchill had taken part in the British Army's last-ever cavalry charge as the British fought to maintain the regime there. The British had had a presence in Egypt for over 60 years, but toward the end of 1951 the families of British servicemen and administrators were evacuated as anti-British rioting in Suez led to violent clashes between British troops and local Egyptian police.

In Australia and New Zealand the royal couple experienced no ill-feeling toward Britain and they travelled extensively through both countries, spending a month in New Zealand and two months in Australia.

When the *Gothic* docked in Auckland and the Queen stepped ashore to be greeted by waiting dignitaries, it was the first time that a reigning monarch had ever visited New Zealand. From the moment she arrived the schedule was relentless, with daily official receptions, functions and visits, including a church service prior to her radio broadcast on Christmas Day. Not until 4 January 1954 did the couple have a break when they spent two days at Moose Lodge, a country house estate set amid a tranquil forest on the shores of Lake Rotoiti. On 6 January they were back on the road, and in the air and on rails for a series of visits to industrial sites, thermal springs, military bases, town halls, hospitals and Maori sites on both North and South Islands.

In the town of Hawera it was decided that some of the buildings on the route to be taken by the royal procession were looking a little shabby. A local schoolteacher subsequently recalled, "Every school child set about making paper flowers in red, white and blue crepe paper." The decorations were used to brighten up the buildings when the Queen drove past.

When the royal couple's car was making its slow and stately progress through the town of Greymouth, one 11-year-old girl detached herself from the crowd and later remembered that "I then ran alongside the car for about half a mile, at which time the Duke of Edinburgh looked across and said, 'If you run much further, you will burst!'"

Whenever they disappeared inside a building, the assembled crowds outside would chant "We want the Queen!" and if that failed to solicit an appearance, they moved on to "We want the duke", which, more often than not, brought the royal couple out onto an appropriate balcony to wave and pose for photographs.

Having arrived at Auckland in the north, the Queen and the duke rejoined *Gothic* in the south, departing from Bluff on 1 April. The one low point of the tour had been a tragedy on Christmas Eve when 151 people were killed in a rail accident, a passenger train having plunged into the Whangaehu River when the bridge collapsed. The Queen expressed her sympathy in her Christmas broadcast and the duke flew to Wellington for the funeral of 21 of the victims on 31 December.

The *Gothic* arrived in Sydney on 3 February and, while the Queen's subjects in Britain shivered in the sub-zero temperatures, snow and gales of a harsh winter, Sydney Harbour basked in the heat of a warm, southern hemisphere summer's day. The harbour was crowded with boats of all shapes and sizes, with people straining for a first glimpse of the country's royal guests. The air was filled with the sound of ship's horns blaring out a welcome, while on shore there was the blast of an artillery salute and in the sky the thunder of jet engines as a formation of RAAF aircraft flew past. The Queen and the duke were ferried ashore from the *Gothic* in the Royal Barge, with small boats forming a wide avenue leading to the landing stage at Farm Cove. Governor-General Sir William Slim and Prime Minister Robert Menzies greeted the Queen as she stepped ashore, before being ushered to an open-topped Daimler limousine to make slow and stately progress along a processional route through the city. A ticker-tape parade and a million well-wishers greeted the royal couple in the streets, setting the tone for the rest of the Australian leg of the tour.

As in New Zealand, this was the first time that a reigning monarch had visited the country, and the schedule was every bit as hectic. They were to visit each of the state capitals, barring Darwin in the Northern Territory, and 70 other towns, travelling by car, train and plane, with the *Gothic* pressed into service for visits to the Barrier Reef and Tasmania, although the royal couple subsequently flew back from Tasmania to the mainland. During the trip they were to cover 10,000 miles (nearly 16,100 kilometres) by air on more than 30 flights – the only way to fit in so many engagements in such a vast country. The engagements included the opening of Parliament in Canberra on a day when the summer weather broke and it poured with rain, although that did not deter the crowds in the streets, and meeting many thousands of service personnel who had fought in both world wars. Wreaths were laid at memorials, a flame was lit at the new forecourt to the Shrine of Remembrance in Melbourne and the Queen was also present for the dedication in Canberra of the 240-foot (73-metre) column topped with a giant eagle that is the Australian-American Memorial that commemorates the help given by the United States during the war in the Pacific.

As well as visits to a "flying doctor" station, military bases, schools and hospitals, there was time for a spot of horse racing at Randwick on 18 April when the Queen watched the inaugural Queen Elizabeth Stakes. After Harry Darwon, the trainer of the winning horse, Blue Ocean, had been presented to the Queen, it was pointed out to him that he had held the sovereign's hand during their handshake rather longer than protocol dictated. While the Queen always enjoyed talking about horses and may well have chatted to Mr Darwon longer than expected, he claimed not to have been clinging on to the monarch but that he was "trembling so much the Queen had to hold my hand to steady me".

The huge enthusiasm and affection shown by the Australian public must have been heartening for the royal couple, although the schedule was gruelling – and while the Queen and Prince Philip continued to grab the headlines, Prime Minister Menzies had more than just the royal visit on his agenda. The shadow of the Cold War was reaching out to

Australia, and a Russian diplomat, Vladimir Petrov (actually a colonel in the KGB), had made contact with the Australian Security Intelligence Organisation (ASIO), arranging to defect and offering details of a Russian spy ring operating in Australia. Petrov's defection eventually happened on 3 April, two days after the Queen had left the country.

But it wasn't only Mr Menzies who was having problems. The demanding round of engagements; the fierce summer heat; the constant smiling and waving; the endless briefings on where they were going and who they were to meet; the handshakes and the pressure to make everyone feel that they were appreciated; the speeches and the official lunches and dinners, were taking their toll on the Queen and the duke. A weekend break had been arranged halfway through the tour at a chalet on the shores of the O'Shanassy Reservoir in the Yarra Ranges, just outside Melbourne. A camera crew was waiting to film the Queen with some kangaroos and koala bears as part of a documentary they were making about the royal tour. The crew was set up outside and waiting patiently, beginning to worry that the light was fading in the late afternoon, when raised voices were heard, coming from the chalet. The raised voices quickly became angry voices and suddenly a door was flung open. The cameraman instinctively flicked the switch to start filming just as the duke hurtled through the door, closely followed by his tennis racquet and shoes. The Queen then appeared, yelling at her husband; then she spotted the camera crew taking an interest and hauled the duke back indoors. Commander Richard Colville, the Queen's press secretary, then approached the camera crew. The documentary film's director, Loch Townsend, offered to hand over the film that had been shot, seeing the continued co-operation of the royal couple with the making of the movie as being more important than some footage of a trivial spat. Shortly afterwards the Queen reappeared and is reported as having thanked the crew for giving up the film, then saying, "I'm sorry for that little interlude but, as you know, it happens in every marriage. Now, what would you like me to do?"

The "little interlude" was reported in an unpublished 1996 thesis on the 1954 Australian tour, *The Glittering Thread*, written by Dr Jane Connors, who had interviewed Loch Townsend. It was published in

Robert Hardman's 2011 biography *Our Queen*. Loch Townsend, who died in 2013, saw his documentary play to packed cinemas for months after the Queen departed from Australia.

On 1 April 1954, the crowds that had cheered the royal couple from Tasmania to the Barrier Reef and from Sydney to the western plains, thronged the quayside at Freemantle to wave goodbye to the Queen and the duke. *Gothic* set sail into the evening sun, leaving Australia behind. But the tour was far from over.

Next stop was the Cocos Islands, albeit a brief visit of only a few hours, before heading on to Ceylon (now Sri Lanka) and Aden (now part of Yemen). Aden was a crown colony that had been of strategic significance to Britain for more than a century. It had been a port where sailing ships travelling between India and Europe could take on water, where later steamships could take on coal and subsequently diesel-powered vessels could refuel. It also became a stopover for British aircraft heading to India and the Far East, and a major oil refinery was established in the port. By the late 1950s it would become one of the busiest ports in the world and the presence of the Royal Navy and RAF in Aden were seen as vital to protecting Britain's oil interests. As a military base it was also ideally positioned to protect the entrance to the Red Sea, leading to the Suez Canal. That would appear to make it an ideal point from which the *Gothic* could make her way up to the Mediterranean, but unrest in Egypt made that an unwise route for the Queen to take. She and the duke flew out of Aden on 28 April, heading for Uganda for a two-day visit before taking to the skies again, this time bound for Tobruk in Libya.

The Queen and the duke flew in to the RAF base at El Adem, visited the cemeteries and memorials to those who had fallen in battle there during the Second World War, inspected British troops stationed in Tobruk and met with King Idris and Queen Fatimah. All of that was, by now, rather routine, but there was something quite extraordinary awaiting them at the end of their Libyan visit: anchored in the warm Mediterranean waters off Tobruk was the newly commissioned royal yacht *Britannia*. Her Majesty's Yacht (HMY) *Britannia* had been ordered the day before the death of King George VI and construction had begun in June 1952. The Duke of Edinburgh was very much involved in the project, revelling in being able to concentrate on a naval enterprise, and the Queen launched the ship at John Brown's shipyard on the Clyde in April 1953. The race was then on to have her ready for her maiden voyage, when she sailed from Portsmouth to Malta with two very important passengers on board.

When the Queen and the duke boarded HMY *Britannia* at Tobruk they were greeted by Prince Charles and Princess Anne, who had travelled from Britain to see their parents for the first time in almost six months. It seems unthinkable to many that their parents should have left such young children behind for so long, but it is a sacrifice that many families, not only royalty, serving in the armed forces have to make from time to time. The reunion, of course, was a joyous one and as *Britannia* headed toward Malta another family member was to join them. Fifteen ships of the Royal Navy's Mediterranean Fleet, led by Admiral Lord Mountbatten in his flagship, formed an escort for *Britannia* and helicopters from the aircraft carrier *Eagle* joined aircraft of the RAF in the sky above the royal yacht.

Four days in Malta were followed by a day in Gibraltar before *Britannia* embarked on a five-day cruise to London and an ecstatic welcome home, where ship's horns and factory sirens blared as the royal yacht sailed up the Thames watched by crowds of waving, cheering well-wishers. During the tour the Queen and the duke had visited 13 countries and covered 43,618 miles (70,196 kilometres) over a period of 172 days. The Queen would never again undertake such a lengthy tour, although she would go on to become the most travelled monarch in history. The coming of the jet age and faster, more efficient road and rail links would make a six-month absence unnecessary.

PRINCESS MARGARET'S DOOMED ROMANCE

On 12 January 1953, in a letter to Sir Alan "Tommy" Lascelles, a trusted confidant who had been private secretary to both King George VI and Queen Elizabeth II, the Queen Mother wrote, "I have really felt quite

Anthony Eden: Victim of Suez

Sir Anthony Eden (he was appointed to the Order of the Garter in 1954) was Britain's prime minister from the time when he succeeded Winston Churchill in April 1955 until his resignation in January 1957.

Born on 12 June 1897 into an aristocratic English family, he was educated at Eton and Oxford, although the First World War delayed his taking up a place at university. During the war he served as an officer with the King's Royal Rifle Corps from late 1915 and was awarded the Military Cross for bravery in action, rescuing a wounded comrade from No Man's Land when a patrol he was leading had become pinned down by enemy fire.

After the war, Eden studied oriental languages at university, having become fluent in both French and German as a child on foreign holidays. He was elected as a Conservative Member of Parliament in 1923 and went on to a career in the Foreign Office. He became Foreign Secretary in 1935 but resigned in 1938 in protest against Prime Minister Neville Chamberlain's policy of appeasement toward Italian dictator Mussolini. He was again Foreign Secretary under Prime Minister Winston Churchill during the Second World War and when Churchill was re-elected in 1951.

Eden married Beatrice Beckett in 1923 and the couple had three sons, one of whom died just 15 minutes after he was born and another was killed in action with the RAF in the Second World War. Eden and Beatrice divorced in 1950 and he married Clarissa Spencer-Churchill in 1952.

Following heavy criticism of his handling of the Suez Crisis, and having become increasingly ill after a series of stomach operations, Eden resigned as prime minister in 1957. He became Earl of Avon in 1961 and died in 1977.

shattered by the whole thing, and cannot help feeling that it would never had happened if the King had been here." The "thing" to which the Queen Mother was referring was the romance between Princess Margaret and Group Captain Peter Townsend. The couple had told her that they intended to marry and the Queen Mother foresaw yet another royal crisis in the making.

Townsend had served as equerry to George VI and was Deputy Master of the Household. These were roles that had brought him into the "inner circle" of those surrounding the royal family ever since he had first been appointed in 1944. He had become an ever-present fixture, a troubleshooter and problem-solver, travelling everywhere with the family.

It was not that he was an employee that was the problem, nor even that he was 15 years older than the princess. He had a distinguished war record, having flown as a fighter pilot in the Battle of Britain, scored 11 "kills" and been shot down twice. He was tall, good-looking and charming, but he was also divorced.

Although Townsend was seen as the "innocent" party, his wife having left him for another man, divorce carried not only a social stigma but also a particular problem when it came to associating with the royal family. At that time, divorcees were not permitted in the royal enclosure at Ascot. Townsend's role as equerry to George VI had not posed a problem because he was not actually divorced until after the king's death.

In a 1949 speech to the Mothers' Union, a Christian charity of which the Queen is still patron, the Queen (then Princess Elizabeth) said: "We can have no doubt that divorce and separation are responsible for some of the darkest evils in society today." The issue had, of course, been at the heart of the abdication crisis in 1936 and the reasons that had made it such a problem then still applied: the monarch is the head of the Church of England, which did not then allow divorcees to marry in church while a previous partner was still alive. As sovereign, although she wanted her sister to be happy, the Queen could not officially condone her marriage to a divorced man.

Under the Royal Marriages Act of 1772, the princess could not marry without the sovereign's consent until she was 25 years old. Even then, Princess Margaret would need permission from Parliament to marry in a civil ceremony and Prime Minister Winston Churchill told the Queen that the Commonwealth heads of state were against the marriage and that Parliament would not give its approval unless Princess Margaret renounced her rights to the throne. As she was only 23, the couple accepted that their marriage would have to wait.

Matters were brought to a head when reporters covering the Queen's coronation spotted Princess Margaret picking a piece of fluff from Townsend's uniform. This was far from normal behaviour for a royal, and there was immediate speculation that the two were romantically linked. In fact, their romance may secretly have begun as long ago as the royal family's 1947 tour to South Africa. By mid-June, the royal romance was hot news and, just as had happened in 1936, a huge portion of the population was of the opinion that Princess Margaret, who was only third in line to the throne after all, should be allowed to marry the man she loved. Townsend was posted to Brussels as a military attaché at the British Embassy. Parliament hoped that waiting out the two-year period in separation might lead to the relationship cooling off. That did not happen, but when faced with the problem again following Princess Margaret's 25th birthday, the couple decided that their future happiness was in serious doubt if so many hurdles were to be put in their way. Princess Margaret issued an official statement on 31 October 1955:

I would like it to be known that I have decided not to marry Group Captain Peter Townsend. I have been aware that, subject to my renouncing my rights of succession, it might have been possible for me to contract a civil marriage. But mindful of the Church's teachings that Christian marriage is indissoluble, and conscious of my duty to the Commonwealth, I have resolved to put these considerations before others.

Four years later Peter Townsend was to marry Marie-Luce Jamagne, who was 24 years his junior and looked remarkably like Princess Margaret.

THE SUEZ CRISIS

A crisis of a different kind hogged the headlines in 1956. When Gamal Abdel Nasser had come to power in Egypt in 1954, he harboured ambitions to become a leader of great influence in the Middle East and he believed that one way of doing this was to attack Israel. Armed incursions into Israel from Syria and Jordan were prompting the Israelis to respond with reprisal attacks, which led to even more deaths. The border skirmishes, coupled with the Egyptians' habit of searching ships and confiscating cargo passing through the Suez Canal bound either to or from Israel, brought the two countries to the brink of war.

Nasser was also at the centre of friction between Egypt, Britain and France. Britain had a huge military base at Suez, from where its 80,000 troops could protect the Suez Canal. The canal had been built by the French in the nineteenth century, opening in 1869, but it was jointly owned by the British and the French through the Suez Canal Company. An international convention of 1888 declared the canal a neutral zone through which international shipping could pass freely at all times. British troops were there to enforce the agreement and, although France actually held the majority of shares in the canal, Britain had physical control of the canal and the running of the Suez Canal Company.

By the 1950s, however, the British troops were seen as an occupation force by militant Egyptians and there were increasing tensions. In January 1952 there was a pitched battle when British forces tried to disarm an Egyptian police unit and 40 Egyptians died. The subsequent civil unrest led to the revolution that brought Nasser into power. As part of a deal to foster good relations between Egypt and Britain, in October 1954 Foreign Secretary Anthony Eden ratified an agreement that would see the gradual withdrawal of British troops from Egypt over a period of 20 months.

In July 1956 Nasser "nationalized" the Suez Canal. With no substantial British force to stop them, his troops seized control of the canal and the Suez Canal Company. Foreign employees of the company were threatened with imprisonment should they attempt either to resign or to leave Egypt. Almost two-thirds of Europe's oil passed through the canal, making it of vital economic importance, and Anthony Eden, by now prime minister, along with his French counterpart Guy Mollet, eventually decided to retake the canal by force.

However, the secret plot that they hatched was far from straight-forward. They wanted the canal and to get rid of Nasser but they did not

Gamal Abdel Nasser: Hero of Egypt

Gamal Abdel Nasser was born the son of a postal worker in Alexandria in 1918. His father's work meant that the family regularly moved from place to place and when he was running a post office in Khatatba, around 30 miles (48 kilometres) north of Cairo, Nasser was sent to live with an uncle in order that he could attend school in the capital. In 1928 he was sent to Alexandria to live with his grandfather, again in order to further his education, but a year later he was back in Alexandria, living with his father (his mother having died in 1926 giving birth to one of Nasser's three brothers). When he was just 15, Nasser became involved in a demonstration by the Young Egypt Society against colonialism and was arrested, spending a night in custody. The Young Egypt Society's paramilitary "Green Shirts" modelled themselves on the German Nazi "Brownshirts". Two years later, Nasser was at the forefront of a demonstration against British rule where two protesters were killed and Nasser had a lucky escape when he was slightly wounded by a bullet that grazed his head.

Nasser applied to Egypt's Royal Military Academy in 1937 but his political activities as a student and police record led to his rejection. He studied law at the King Faud University in Cairo for a year before re-applying to the military academy and being accepted. He achieved national acclaim for his actions in the Arab–Israeli war of 1948 but his hunger for change in his country had not abated.

He was instrumental in establishing the clandestine Free Officers Movement within the Egyptian Army. When 40 Egyptian police officers were killed during a clash with British forces in Ismailia in 1952, followed by the deaths of 76 demonstrators in riots in Cairo the next day, the Free Officers decided to move against the corrupt King Farouk and the country's political elite. The coup was a success but political unrest continued, with Nasser very much to the fore. He became Egypt's prime minister in 1954 and the country's president in 1956, surviving a 1954 assassination attempt along the way. He remained as president for 26 years through huge turmoil in the Middle East, including defeat in the 1967 Six Day War with Israel, after which he temporarily resigned. Nasser died from a massive heart attack (his third) in 1970.

want it to look like they had deposed an Arab leader because that would cause severe problems with other Arab states. Nasser was denying Israel access to the canal, and Eden and Mollet decided to work with the Israelis. The plan was for Israel to invade the Sinai Peninsula and for Britain and France to then move in, occupy Port Said and the canal zone as peacekeepers to separate the two warring factions and secure the canal for international trade.

Following Israel's lead, British and French troops invaded on 29 October 1956, but the whole plan came unstuck when the UN and the USA would not support the Anglo-French invasion. The USA even threatened economic sanctions against Britain. Although they were successfully achieving their military objectives, the invaders were ordered to cease fire and were withdrawn in December. The Egyptians suffered thousands of casualties in the action, with at least 1,000 civilians dead. Casualties among the invading forces were comparatively light but there was still outrage in Britain that the country had been dragged into yet another war. In Parliament, the political pressure on Anthony Eden was intense, especially as he was found to have misled the House of Commons when he stated that he and Guy Mollet had no foreknowledge of the planned Israeli attack. With his reputation severely tarnished, Prime Minister Anthony Eden resigned in January 1957. Harold Macmillan replaced him, the Queen's third prime minister in five years. In the whole of his 16 years as king, her father had known only four.

CHAPTER SIX

FAMILY & DUTY

Britain forged ahead into the 1960s with industry booming, wartime rationing a thing of the past and National Service in the armed forces officially ending in December 1960. This meant young men were more at liberty to live life to the full and enjoy themselves. They could also quite literally let their hair down as longer hair became fashionable for men, while shorter skirts were all the rage for women. British fashion designer Mary Quant championed the mini skirt, while The Beatles and the Rolling Stones were leading the way for British pop and rock music to blaze a trail on the international scene. This was also the dawn of the jet age, when new airliners made it possible for British workers to take holidays in Mediterranean resorts in Spain, France or Italy rather than in the traditional seaside towns like Blackpool, Margate or Bognor.

Yet amid the energetic optimism for the future, the Cold War still cast a chill of dark shadows into every corner of the world. NATO and the Soviet Bloc forces faced each other over a border in a divided Germany – a border that also divided Europe. The whole world held its breath when the USA and the USSR came close to direct military conflict when

Soviet nuclear missiles were based in Cuba in 1962. British fighter jets intercepted Soviet aircraft probing British air space two or three times every week. In Vietnam, American troops fought alongside their allies against communist forces from North Vietnam, which were backed by the USSR and China. In the Middle East, Egypt (armed by the USSR) led the Arab nations in clashes with Israel (armed by the USA). Where the Cold War turned hot, there was an ever-present danger of an escalation that ultimately – given the terrifying power of the nuclear arsenals now held by the USA, USSR, Britain, China and France – could destroy the entire planet.

For the British royal family, tensions around the globe – and the fact that the brave new world of the 1960s encouraged ever more of Britain's territories, colonies and dependencies abroad to seek independence – made the royal diplomatic role more important than ever. At home, as television, radio, newspapers and magazines became increasingly intrusive, always anxious to be first with the latest royal story, the Queen and her family had little choice but to acknowledge their celebrity and adopt a new attitude toward the media.

HOME AND AWAY

While Britain plunged headlong into the bold and brash colour, innovation and excitement of the 1960s, the Queen approached the new decade at a more sedate pace. She was still a relatively young woman, in her mid-30s, but the new fashions were certainly not for her.

When relaxing at Sandringham, walking her dogs in the countryside or stalking in the hills around Balmoral, she was most likely to be seen in tweeds or waterproofs with stout walking shoes. When she was working, which was most of the time, she had a "uniform". Wherever she went crowds would gather to see her and she acknowledged that it was part of her job to be seen. This meant that hats could not have too wide a brim and clothes needed to be elegant yet practical. Weights were discreetly sewn into the hemlines of her skirts to prevent gusts of wind, frequently a problem at airports, causing any embarrassment. The Queen chose to wear pastel colours that were not so bold as to be vulgar, yet would still help her to stand out against a crowd, again helping her to be seen.

The domestic visits opening factories, hospitals or new municipal buildings were just part of her job. Another task was setting aside time each day to review her "red box" papers to keep herself up to date with affairs of state. As Princess Elizabeth, the Queen had studied history and the British constitution in years of private lessons with Sir Henry Marten, the Provost of Eton College. She was an expert on the constitution and read the official papers in order that she might offer advice to her government, but also so that she was fully informed about domestic and foreign issues in preparation for official engagements. She once described how, "The boxes and communications just keep on coming and with modern communications they come even quicker. Luckily I'm a quick reader and I can get through quite a lot of reading in a short time." Successive governments came to refer to her as "Reader Number One".

The Queen's role as an international stateswoman took her all over the world, making her the most travelled monarch in history. In 1957 Ghana became the first of Britain's colonies to become independent. During the 1960s Ghana was followed by Nigeria, Sierra Leone, Tanganyika (Tanzania), Uganda, Kenya, Malawi and Northern Rhodesia (Zambia). The Queen visited more than three dozen countries during the 1960s, as far apart as New Zealand and West Germany, or Pakistan and the Bahamas. These included nations such as Liberia, Ethiopia, The Gambia and Ghana, where keeping her safe was not always easy. When she was due to visit Canada in October 1964, there had been reports that extremists in the Quebec separatist movement, who had been planting bombs in a terror campaign, were intent on assassinating the Queen. Mindful of events in Dallas the previous November, the Queen was advised to cancel the trip but she refused, seeing it as her duty to undertake the trip. Backing out would have made her, and the monarchy, look bad.

The Queen was not alone in undertaking extensive foreign trips. For the most part, she was accompanied by her husband, but he also undertook solo missions. In 1956 he was away for four months, opening the Olympics in Melbourne and visiting far-flung places such as the

Falkland Islands and St Helena. In 1959 he was in India, Pakistan and the Pacific Islands, while in the 1960s he visited the USA and South America. By then he was HRH Prince Philip, the Duke of Edinburgh, the Queen having made him a British prince in 1957.

John F. Kennedy: The USA's Youngest President

John Fitzgerald Kennedy, known as "Jack" or "JFK", was born in Brookline, Massachusetts, on 29 May 1917. He came from a wealthy family and his father was a businessman and politician, serving at one time as the American ambassador in London.

Although his early education was interrupted by intermittent stomach ailments, JFK studied at Harvard, graduating in 1940. When he applied to train as an officer in the US Army, he was rejected due to lower back problems but he exercised to strengthen his back and was eventually accepted into the United States Naval Reserve. During the Second World War he served at first in naval intelligence but was later transferred to a torpedo boat squadron. His back was injured when a Japanese destroyer sank his boat and he was awarded the Navy and Marine Corps Medal for bravery in saving one of his injured crew. He retired from the US Navy due to continuing back problems in 1945, and would be plagued by back pain and stomach disorders for the rest of his life.

In 1947 JFK followed his father into politics and served in the House of Representatives until 1953, when he was elected Senator of Massachusetts. He also married Jacqueline Bouvier in 1953 and the couple had four children, Arabella, Caroline, John and Patrick, although JFK is known to have had a string of extra-marital relationships. In January 1961 he succeeded Eisenhower as President of the USA at the age of 43.

JFK's presidency is best known for his support of the Civil Rights Movement, his handling of the Cuban Missile Crisis and, tragically, his assassination by a gunman in Dallas on 22 November 1963. Lee Harvey Oswald was arrested for the murder but was shot by nightclub owner Jack Ruby before he could stand trial, sparking suspicions of a conspiracy and cover-up that continue to this day.

Princess Margaret also undertook independent official tours, most notably to Jamaica in 1962 when she represented the Crown at the island's independence ceremony and, not to be left out, the Queen Mother, a sprightly 60-year-old in 1960, undertook some lengthy tours. In May 1960 she wrote to Princess Margaret from Northern Rhodesia, describing the Barotseland territory: "The old Paramount Chief is a good ruler and nobody can approach him except on their knees! I think we might introduce this at Clarence House..."

FAMILY AFFAIRS

In 1960 Princess Margaret married society photographer Antony Armstrong-Jones. The couple had met through friends at a dinner party in 1958, and by 1959 their romance, although still a secret, was blossoming. The princess wrote to London-based Armstrong-Jones from Balmoral in August 1959 telling him how happy she was and that she had "left London tremendously NOT in turmoil", indicating that the turmoil of her relationship with Peter Townsend was well and truly over.

The couple were to have two children, David (born in November 1961) and Sarah (born in May 1964). Armstrong-Jones was the first commoner to marry a British royal princess for four centuries so, in order that his children would have suitable titles, he was created Earl Snowdon and Viscount Linley in October 1961.

The Queen's family was also expanding. In February 1960 her second son, Prince Andrew Albert Christian Edward, was born and in March 1964 Prince Edward Antony Richard Louis came along. By that time the Queen was almost 38 years old, considered a little old to be giving birth in the 1960s – and even today would be termed a "geriatric mother" or of "advanced maternal age", terms used by medical staff to alert them to the fact that they are not dealing with someone in their teens or 20s. In any case, all went smoothly and Prince Philip telephoned Prince Charles, at school at Gordonstoun in Scotland, and Princess Anne, at school at Benenden in Kent, to tell them that they had a baby brother.

The Queen and Prince Philip had decided that their children should be given as "normal" an upbringing as was humanly possible. They could never do things that most people take for granted – they could never walk out of their front door to meet friends in the park or to go shopping, but neither were they to have quite as sheltered an existence as had the Queen and Princess Margaret.

Prince Charles first went to school at Hill House in West London and then to Cheam School in Berkshire. Prince Philip had also attended the school, and Prince Charles was also to follow his father to Gordonstoun School in Moray, Scotland, despite the Queen Mother pleading for him to be sent to Eton, closer to home. Prince Philip was determined that his son should be exposed to the demanding regime at Gordonstoun that had served him well, but Prince Charles was a more sensitive child than his father had been and, at first, hated Gordonstoun. The emphasis was on building a resilient character through physical challenges as much as it was on academic prowess and Prince Charles referred to it as "Colditz in kilts". Prince Charles saw it through, albeit with two of his school terms spent at Timbertop (part of Geelong Grammar School in Victoria, Australia), eventually becoming Guardian, the school's version of Head Boy. He left Gordonstoun in 1967 and later said that the school had done him good, although he enjoyed Timbertop far more.

Princess Anne had a little more of the upbringing that her mother and aunt had experienced as the Buckingham Palace Guide Company was re-formed to allow her to associate with other girls of her age. She was a more robust character than her older brother and not above picking fights with him should he, for example, happen to be playing with a toy that she wanted – much like most other brothers and sisters. Princess Anne was educated at first by a tutor but at the age of 13 she was sent to Benenden, a boarding school in Kent – a first for any daughter of a British monarch. She was good at sports, especially tennis and lacrosse, but excelled on horseback, and riding became her passion.

Whenever possible, the Queen liked to make time for her children, even bringing forward her weekly meeting with her prime minister so that she could be there for bedtime when Andrew and Edward were little. Both boys had a governess who was responsible for the first stage of their schooling, but both also went to Heatherdown School in Berkshire before progressing, as their father and older brother had done, to Gordonstoun. Prince Andrew was to spend six months of his time at Gordonstoun on an exchange course to Lakefield College School in Canada, while Prince Edward spent a couple of terms working as a teacher at Wanganui Collegiate School in New Zealand after leaving Gordonstoun.

In 1958 Prince Charles had been created Prince of Wales and Earl of Chester, which may not have meant much to a young boy not yet 10 years old but in 1969, as he approached his 21st birthday, he was well able to understand that "Prince of Wales" was the title given to the male heir to the throne – the man who would be king. His investiture as Prince of Wales took place at Caernarfon Castle on 1 July 1969. The prince spent weeks leading up to the investiture learning about Welsh history and the Welsh language so that he could speak in English and Welsh during the ceremony.

Three days after his investiture, Prince Charles received a letter from Lord Mountbatten offering him some advice. Mountbatten had been a valued counsellor and uncle to Prince Philip when he was a young man and now strove to help the new Prince of Wales focus on his responsibilities by pointing out to him where the previous Prince of Wales had gone wrong. Mountbatten wrote: "Realise how fickle public support can be. Your uncle David had such popularity that he thought he could flout the government and the church and make a twice-divorced woman queen. His popularity disappeared overnight."

THE TROUBLES

Although the Queen helped to promote British interests and international unity throughout the former British Empire in her role as head of the swiftly growing Commonwealth, she could do little more than watch when violence flared at home in the United Kingdom. Problems that had existed for decades in Northern Ireland began to bubble over into violence in the mid-1960s. Various groups campaigned for equal and fair civil rights in the province and some were nationalists or republicans, who wanted Northern Ireland and the Republic of Ireland (Eire) in the south to be reunited as one country. Eire is a predominantly Catholic country and the minority nationalists in Northern Ireland were also predominantly Catholic. Northern Ireland, however, is predominantly (by a smaller margin) Protestant and the "loyalists" who wanted to remain part of the United Kingdom were predominantly Protestant. Thus the political divide was also a religious sectarian divide and the enmity between the two sides stretched back to the Irish War of Independence (1919–21) and the partition of the island in 1921. Eire was an independent republic with its own government whereas Northern Ireland had been created at partition to remain as part of the United Kingdom, although it also had its own government. From 1963 to 1969 Northern Ireland's prime minister was Terence O'Neill, leader of the Ulster Unionist Party.

The civil rights issues included complaints about the way that Catholics were treated in the workplace. There was widespread discrimination, with fewer jobs available to Catholics, including jobs with any official status such as the civil service or local government posts. As far as the Catholics were concerned, the best jobs always went to Protestants.

With government jobs taken mainly by Protestants, Catholics were pushed further down the queue when it came to local authority housing. Protestants rather than Catholics were given council houses when they became available. With fewer job opportunities, the Catholic population also tended to be less wealthy than the Protestants, causing issues when it came to voting. In Northern Ireland only property-owners could vote, although in the rest of the United Kingdom all adults were allowed to vote. In Northern Ireland, if you could not afford to buy a house or you did not own your own business, you were ineligible to vote. This, of course, disenfranchised many and put political power mainly in the hands of the Protestant loyalists.

These and other grievances, including sectarianism and discrimination within the police force, the Royal Ulster Constabulary (RUC), led to protest marches and clashes between nationalists and loyalists. Amid claims that the nationalists were being led by a resurgent Irish Republican Army (IRA), which had been relatively inactive for some time, loyalists formed the Ulster Volunteer Force (UVF). They declared war on the IRA and all of its so-called sympathizers. Violence began to escalate with a series of murders, bombings and retaliations by the different factions.

In January 1969, a four-day march between Belfast and Londonderry, organized by a group of student civil rights activists, became the focus for numerous violent incidents, culminating in a heavy-handed operation by the RUC in the Bogside area of Londonderry. Catholic residents in Bogside sealed off the streets leading into the area, using vehicles as barricades, and proclaimed a "Free Derry", refusing entry to the RUC. Violent clashes continued over the ensuing months and bomb attacks left parts of Belfast with no water or electricity. The British government sent troops to guard key installations; with the violence and terrorist attacks seeming to have spiralled out of control, Terence O'Neill resigned.

In August 1969 the RUC used armoured vehicles, tear gas and water cannon in an attempt to overrun Bogside. Hundreds of nationalists fought with police for two days in what became known as the Battle of the Bogside. Rioting and fighting between nationalists and loyalists also broke out in Belfast, and Eire's prime minister announced that he was ordering the Irish Army to set up medical posts for refugees on the border. He called for the United Nations to intervene and even secretly considered plans for the Irish Army to invade Northern Ireland as a peacekeeping force. In the middle of August, the British government sent in troops to patrol the streets and restore order in Londonderry and Belfast. For a time, things settled down but eight people had been shot dead, more than 130 had bullet wounds and over 600 more had been badly injured. The British Army was welcomed at first, trusted by both nationalists and loyalists to keep the peace, but the harmony was not to last long.

Harold Wilson: A Different Sort of Prime Minister

Labour Party leader Harold Wilson became British prime minister in 1964 after the ruling Conservative Party had been rocked by two damaging sex scandals. The first was the 1962 revelation that John Vassall, a civil servant at the Admiralty in London, was passing sensitive military information to the Soviets who were blackmailing him over previous homosexual liaisons in Moscow. The second scandal was the infamous "Profumo Affair", when 47-year-old married Secretary of State for War John Profumo denied having an affair with 19-year-old model Christine Keeler, who had also been sleeping with Captain Yevgeny Ivanov, the Soviet naval attaché. Profumo had lied to Parliament and was forced to resign. Prime Minister Harold Macmillan, citing health problems, also stood down on 19 October 1963. Macmillan's successor, Alec Douglas-Home, had just 12 months to prepare for the 1964 General Election. Harold Wilson's Labour Party eventually ended 13 years of Tory rule with a narrow win.

Harold Wilson was unlike any of the Queen's previous prime ministers. Born James Harold Wilson on 11 March 1916 in Huddersfield, Yorkshire, his father was an industrial chemist and his mother a teacher. He won a scholarship to grammar school and then studied at Oxford University (becoming an Oxford don at only 21). He spent most of his adult life working in London but never lost his gritty Yorkshire accent. To Queen Elizabeth II, he would immediately have sounded totally different from the procession of Harrow- and Eton-educated aristocrats who had preceded him.

During the Second World War, Wilson volunteered for military service but was assigned to the civil service where he worked as a statistician. In 1945 he was elected as a Labour MP and won a place in Clement Attlee's government. Appointed President of the Board of Trade in 1947, at 31 he was the youngest Cabinet member of any government in the twentieth century.

When Labour was voted out of office in 1951, Wilson held various posts in the Shadow Cabinet, becoming Labour leader in 1963. Following the 1964 election, he remained as prime minister until 1970, notably refusing pressure from the USA to provide military assistance in Vietnam. He became prime minister again in 1974 and held a referendum on whether to remain part of the European Economic Community (EEC). The British public voted to stay. He resigned in 1976, perhaps already aware that he was suffering from early-onset Alzheimer's disease. The Queen came to a retirement dinner in Downing Street, something she had only ever done before for Winston Churchill.

Wilson married once, to Mary Baldwin, and the couple had two sons, Robin and Giles. He died in 1995, aged 79.

CHAPTER SEVEN

THE MONARCHY:
A RAY OF HOPE

Britain in the 1970s witnessed industrial unrest, recession, unemployment, terrorist violence and the prospect of a bleak future, yet through it all the Queen and the royal family carried on, demonstrating to the nation that, whatever happened, Britain would survive.

The situation in Northern Ireland deteriorated dramatically. The death toll rose into the thousands and terrorist bombs were planted in many mainland cities, including Glasgow, Manchester, Liverpool, Coventry, Bristol and Southampton. In London, King's Cross and Euston stations were bombed, as were the Houses of Parliament. Airey Neave MP was killed in 1979 when his car was blown up as he drove out of the Palace of Westminster car park. On 30 January 1972 disturbances in the Bogside area of Londonderry led to soldiers of the Parachute Regiment, who maintained that they had come under fire, shooting dead 14 demonstrators – a day that became known as "Bloody Sunday". On 21 July that year, following a relentless series of violent incidents and bombings, 22 bombs were detonated in Belfast in less than an hour and a half. Nine people died and 130 were wounded.

Economic recession forced the British government to impose a pay freeze, resulting in strikes, power cuts, uncollected rubbish piling up in the streets and a three-day working week when businesses closed to save energy. In 1973 the Arab nations of the Organization of the Petroleum Exporting Countries (OPEC) imposed an embargo on supplies to any country supporting Israel in its war against a coalition of Arab states led by Egypt and Syria. Fuel shortages led to long queues at petrol stations. The embargo drove up oil prices and was a major factor in the onset of recession.

In the Commonwealth countries, political power struggles brought armed conflict, not least in Rhodesia. Having declared independence in 1965, Rhodesia became the Republic of Rhodesia in 1970 and a bitter civil war erupted that continued throughout the 1970s until the country became Zimbabwe, with Robert Mugabe its first president.

For the Queen, these problems were to be eclipsed by events both joyous and tragic during the course of the decade. She dealt with all of the ups and downs with composure and dignity, providing an element of stability and reassurance that gave everyone hope for the future.

DEFIANTLY ON DISPLAY

While the personal security of the Queen and other members of the royal family was always a major concern for the security services and the police personal protection officers (PPOs), it became even more of a headache in 1970 when, to further increase her visibility and meet more people on official visits, the Queen adopted a "walkabout" policy. The people of Wellington, New Zealand, claim that the first walkabout took place when the Queen and Prince Philip, along with Prince Charles and Princess Anne, visited in March 1970. When the royal party arrived by car at the town hall, rather than being whisked straight inside without any of the assembled well-wishers catching a glimpse of them, they got out of the car nearby and walked through the crowds, stopping to chat from time to time.

Other places, notably Valetta in Malta, maintain that they were treated to walkabouts prior to the Wellington visit, but from 1970 onwards it became an important part of a royal visit, with the Queen and Prince Philip often "working" opposite sides of the street to meet as many people as possible. Other royal couples have subsequently followed suit. In terms of security, this left the Queen starkly exposed close to a milling crowd of unknown people – any security officer's worst nightmare. The Queen, however, believed that those who had made the effort to come to see her, or possibly exchange a few words, should be able to do just that.

So it was that on a sunny day on 20 November 1972, for the grand procession through the streets of the capital to Westminster Abbey for the Thanksgiving Service to celebrate the Queen and Prince Philip's 25th wedding anniversary, the Queen, Prince Philip, Prince Charles and Princess Anne rode in the open state landau, drawn by four immaculate grey horses. They were preceded and followed by mounted squadrons of the Household Cavalry, looking hugely impressive in full regalia, but there were no PPOs in sight. When the landau paused for a few minutes, while the official ceremony of the monarch asking permission from the mayor to enter the City of London took place, all four royals sat chatting, smiling and waving to the crowds that lined the streets. They were quite literally sitting targets and it is a situation that would be unthinkable for any US president – yet the Queen insists on being seen.

Following the service, there was a luncheon at Guildhall, when the Queen gave a speech in which she recalled being asked by a bishop what she thought of sin. She said, "I am against it." She then said that, "If I am asked today what I think about family life after 25 years of marriage I can answer with equal simplicity and conviction. I am for it." Silver wedding presents arrived from around the world, perhaps the most unusual of which was the gift from the President of Cameroon – Jumbo, a baby African elephant. Jumbo went to the children's zoo at Crystal Palace.

Making the royal family more accessible to the public was a strategy that had been followed for some years and had met with success. The royals had to cope with being the centre of media attention in a world where their celebrity made everything that they did, everywhere that they went and everything that they wore big news. The Queen had been addressing the nation on television since the broadcast of her 1957 Christmas message. At first she had to cope with the stress of a live broadcast but from 1959 it was pre-recorded, so on Christmas Day at 3 p.m., the royal family gathers round the television at Sandringham to watch, just as millions of others do all over the country. From 1967 the broadcast was in colour but there was no message in 1969 because the Queen felt that the televised investiture of the Prince of Wales, along with a feature-length "behind the scenes" documentary, *Royal Family*, had probably given the public enough of her family that year. Clips from *Royal Family* surface from time to time but the Queen controls the broadcast rights in documentary and it has never again been screened in its entirety.

On 14 November 1973 there was no holding back for the biggest royal televised event to that date: the marriage of Princess Anne to cavalry officer Lieutenant Mark Phillips. The couple had met through their shared interest in horses and had both competed in events at international level. In 1971 Princess Anne had won the individual title at the European Eventing Championship, also becoming BBC Sports Personality of the Year. She was to remain part of the British eventing team and won silver medals in individual and team disciplines at the 1975 European Eventing Championship. In 1976 she was part of the British equestrian team at the Olympic Games in Montreal.

Lieutenant Phillips was a "commoner", although his grandfather had been an aide-de-camp to King George VI. He was commissioned as an officer in the Queen's Dragoon Guards in 1969 and was, naturally, an expert equestrian. He won the Badminton Horse Trials in 1971, 1972, 1974 and 1981, as well as being part of the British equestrian team that won a gold medal at the 1972 Olympic Games in Munich.

On the day of her wedding, just as it had done almost exactly a year before for her parents' Silver Wedding anniversary, there was bright winter sunshine. Princess Anne left Buckingham Palace with her father in a coach escorted by the Household Cavalry through streets lined with cheering crowds all the way to Westminster Abbey. Attempting to insist that there was not too much fuss over the wedding, Princess Anne had limited her attendants to her nine-year-old brother, Prince Edward, as a page boy, and her nine-year-old cousin, Lady Sarah Armstrong-Jones, as a bridesmaid. The fuss, however, was unavoidable.

At 22 years of age, Princess Anne was the young, glamorous face of the royal family and there had been huge speculation in the media about what the royal wedding dress would look like. It was kept a strict secret, despite 15 dressmakers working on it – each being given a different job with none knowing how the complete design would look. The dress, designed by Maureen Baker, was finally revealed when Princess Anne stepped out of the carriage at Westminster Abbey. It was a Tudor-style dress embroidered with pearls, a high neck and long, "trumpet" sleeves. The royal occasion, as such events had done before, proved to be a tonic for the British people, with countless thousands lining the processional route to the abbey and clamouring at the gates of Buckingham Palace for the traditional balcony appearance. The entire event was broadcast on television with a worldwide audience of at least 100 million.

Princess Anne hit the headlines around the world again in March 1974 when a gunman attempted to kidnap her in The Mall in London. The princess and her husband were returning to Buckingham Palace from a charity film screening along with Princess Anne's lady-in-waiting Rowena Brassey and her PPO Inspector James Beaton. The chauffeur of their limousine was one of the royal household's drivers, Alex Callender. The Mall was quiet at that time of the evening but a car suddenly cut in front of the limousine, forcing it to a halt. Beaton got out of the car, believing that he was about to deal with some sort of road rage incident, and saw the driver of the other vehicle coming toward him with a gun in each hand. Before he could draw his own weapon, he was shot. He managed to draw his Walther PPK and fired one shot at the attacker, although his aim was off due to his wound. His weapon then jammed. Alex Callender then attempted to disarm the gunman and was also shot. The gunman reached the limousine and tried to open the door while the princess and her husband held it closed. Rowena Brassey slipped out of the car on the opposite side and took cover as Inspector Beaton pushed his way between the gunman and the princess. He was shot in the hand and again in the abdomen.

A newspaper reporter, Brian McConnell, who had come over to see what the fuss was about, tried to remonstrate with the gunman but was immediately shot. The gunman demanded that the princess get out of the car, to which her response was "Not bloody likely", and then a passing pedestrian, former boxer Ron Russell, rushed the gunman, punching him in the head. While he was disoriented, Russell led the princess, who had dived out of the car on the opposite side, to safety just as a police officer, PC Michael Hills – reacting to the sound of gunfire, arrived and tackled the gunman. He too was shot, but not before he used his radio to call for back-up. When he realized that more police were arriving, the gunman fled but was spotted by Detective Constable Peter Edmonds who chased him down, subdued and arrested him.

The gunman, Ian Ball, was not a terrorist but had planned the kidnap in order to hold the princess to ransom. He was deemed mentally unstable and was imprisoned in the high-security psychiatric facility at Broadmoor. All of those who were shot survived their injuries. Callender, McConnell and Edmonds were awarded the Queen's Gallantry Medal, Hills and Russell were awarded the George Medal and Beaton received the George Cross. At the presentation ceremony, the Queen is reported to have said to him, "The medal is from the Queen, the thank you is from a mother."

Unlike so many other prominent figures, the Queen and the royal family are not difficult to track down because their engagements are published as a schedule of events in the Court Circular. Despite the fact that the royals are high-profile targets for terrorists or disturbed personalities like Ian Ball, they see it as their job to be on show to promote the events and causes that they support, so they remain defiantly on display.

THE SILVER JUBILEE

During the 1970s, the Queen visited around 50 foreign countries throughout the world, with 1977 reserved for Commonwealth countries as part of her Silver Jubilee celebrations. In the spring she toured the Pacific islands of Western Samoa, Tonga, Fiji and Papua New Guinea, as well as Australia and New Zealand, and in the autumn she visited Canada, the Bahamas, the British Virgin Islands, Antigua and Barbados. That left the summer to spend at home. Normally, "at home" during the summer

Edward Heath: The Musical Prime Minister

Born in Broadstairs in Kent on 9 July 1916, Edward Richard George Heath attended Chatham House Grammar School in Ramsgate before progressing to Oxford University in 1935. He graduated with a degree in Philosophy, Politics and Economics in 1939.

After war was declared, he served as an officer in the Royal Artillery, at first with an anti-aircraft unit in Liverpool but later in command of a battery during the Normandy landings and in subsequent actions in France and Germany.

After the war he worked as a civil servant in the Ministry of Civil Aviation but stood as Conservative MP for Bexley in 1950. Heath rose steadily through the party ranks and was Minister of Labour in 1959 before becoming Lord Privy Seal in 1960 and overseeing the negotiations for Britain's entry into the European Economic Community (EEC), subsequently vetoed by President Charles de Gaulle. Although the Conservatives were voted out of office in 1964, Heath retained his seat and became leader of the Conservative Party in 1965.

The Conservatives were voted back into power in the General Election of 1970 with Heath as prime minister. Heath presided over the introduction of decimal currency in 1971 and eventually took Britain into the EEC in 1973, but it was a hugely troubled period in Britain and he was also responsible for the suspension of the Parliament in Northern Ireland, introducing what was known as "direct rule" from London in an attempt to control the warring factions in the province.

It was also a time of economic recession with two damaging miners' strikes having resulted in the "three-day week". In the 1974 election, Harold Wilson's Labour Party won just four more seats than the Conservatives and, despite attempts to forge an alliance with the Liberal Party, Heath was forced out of office.

In 1975 Margaret Thatcher ousted Heath as leader of the Conservative Party and he was ever thereafter one of her strongest critics. He was created a Knight of the Garter in 1992, becoming Sir Edward Heath, and continued to serve as an MP until his retirement in 2001.

Heath was also known as a competitive yachtsman. Having bought his first yacht, *Morning Cloud*, in 1969, he was captain of the 1971 British team in the prestigious Admiral's Cup regatta, winning the trophy. He was also a talented musician, conducting a number of world-class orchestras that included the London Symphony Orchestra and the Royal Liverpool Philharmonic. Sir Edward Heath died on 17 July 2005, aged 89.

means Balmoral, which the Queen regards as her summer residence. During an average week she is at Buckingham Palace, at the weekends she is at Windsor Castle, over Christmas she is at Sandringham and in the summer she is at Balmoral. She once said of her summer in Scotland that, "To be able to sleep in the same bed for six weeks is a nice change."

This year, however, the Queen was not to enjoy any such relaxation. She attended events throughout the UK during the summer, from the launch of London Transport's Silver Jubilee buses to the launch of the aircraft carrier HMS *Invincible* in Barrow-in-Furness. Travelling throughout the country, of course, also meant visiting Northern Ireland. When it was suggested that the situation there might make it best to forgo a visit, the Queen would hear none of it. She visited Belfast and Londonderry in August.

On the evening of 6 June, the Queen lit a Jubilee bonfire beacon at Windsor Castle that triggered the lighting of a chain of similar beacons, all within sight of each other, across the entire length and breadth of the kingdom. The main event of the Jubilee was on 7 June, which was declared a public holiday. Once again hundreds of thousands turned out to line the streets, some camping out overnight, to see the royal procession from Buckingham Palace to the Jubilee service at St Paul's Cathedral, which was attended by all of the royal family, Prime Minister James Callaghan and all of the living former prime ministers, US President Jimmy Carter and leaders from around the world.

Street parties were organized all over the country, with 4,000 taking place in London alone, and the celebrations, which some had questioned on the grounds of austerity, once again proved that the British people like nothing better than a glittering royal occasion to lift them above the rigours of everyday life.

THE MURDER OF MOUNTBATTEN

Lord Louis Mountbatten, 1st Earl Mountbatten of Burma, had an impeccable royal background. His father, Prince Louis of Battenberg, had married Princess Alice, one of Queen Victoria's granddaughters, and Queen Victoria was one of Mountbatten's godparents. His sister, Princess Alice of Battenberg, was Prince Philip's mother.

Mountbatten was actually born Prince Louis Francis Albert Victor Nicholas of Battenberg. His father had a distinguished career in the Royal Navy, becoming First Lord of the Admiralty prior to the First World War, at which point his German heritage made it necessary for him to retire and the family changed their name to Mountbatten at the same time as King George V changed his family name to Windsor.

Following his father into the Royal Navy, he served aboard the battleships HMS *Lion* and HMS *Queen Elizabeth* during the First World War. In 1939, following various staff postings and engineering studies, he was given command of the destroyer HMS *Kelly* and during the Second World War he was commander of the 5th Destroyer Flotilla. He ended the war with the rank of Rear Admiral and took the Japanese surrender of Singapore in September 1945. He was appointed Viceroy of India in 1947 and oversaw the transfer of power during the Partition of India. Mountbatten was a close confidant to his nephew Prince Philip, guiding his naval career and even giving him his name when Philip had to divest himself of his foreign titles prior to his marriage to Princess Elizabeth. Prince Philip, however, is quick to dispel the belief that Mountbatten was a surrogate father to him, saying, "One thing that needs to be corrected is that I was brought up by Lord Mountbatten... I grew up very much more with my father's family than with my mother's."

Mountbatten was, however, a huge influence on the royal family. He became a mentor to Prince Charles and even tried to persuade Charles to marry his granddaughter, Amanda, who was nine years younger than Charles. The prince did eventually propose in late 1979, but Amanda turned him down.

Perhaps part of the reason for her rejection of Charles was the fact that an IRA bomb planted on his fishing boat had killed her grandfather. Mountbatten had a summer home, Classiebawn Castle in County Sligo, Eire. On 27 August 1979 he took some of his family out on his wooden boat, *Shadow V*. The radio-controlled bomb was detonated a few hundred yards from shore, blowing the boat to pieces. Mountbatten was killed, as were his grandson Nicholas (14) and a local crew member Paul

Maxwell (15). Also aboard were Mountbatten's daughter Patricia (Lady Brabourne), her husband John (Lord Brabourne), John's mother and Nicholas's twin brother Timothy. All were injured and Lord Brabourne's 83-year-old mother subsequently died from her injuries. Having lost her grandfather, her younger brother and her grandmother to a terrorist bomb would surely not have made becoming part of the high-profile royal family an attractive prospect to Amanda.

Lord Mountbatten was given a state funeral at Westminster Abbey on 5 September 1979 with the royal family in attendance and he was later buried in accordance with his wishes at Romsey Abbey near his country home, Broadlands.

THE PALACE SPY

The Royal Collection is one of the most famous and important art collections in the world. Housed in 13 royal residences in the UK, where much of it is on display to the public, it includes jewellery, tapestries, sculptures, clocks, furniture and all manner of works of art. The entire collection amounts to more than a million objects, among which are 7,000 paintings, 30,000 watercolours and around 500,000 prints. Part of the collection is personally owned by the Queen, and part is owned by the Crown. Today the Royal Collection is managed and maintained by the Royal Collection Trust, and within the trust the care of the paintings is the responsibility of the Surveyor of the Queen's Pictures. This is a title that dates back to the beginning of the seventeenth century, although most people in Britain would not have been aware of it until it was mentioned in the House of Commons by Prime Minister Margaret Thatcher on 16 November 1979.

Mrs Thatcher's statement was not about the role of surveyor itself, but about the man who held the title: esteemed art historian Sir Anthony Blunt. Blunt had published a number of highly regarded books on art, architecture and art history, and he was a world-renowned expert on French artist Nicolas Poussin. He was Professor of Art History at the University of London and a director of the Courtauld Institute of Art. He was also a distant relative of the Queen Mother. What was not widely known about him at the time, until it was revealed by Mrs Thatcher, was that he had been a Soviet spy.

Blunt had studied at Cambridge University in the 1920s and 1930s, becoming involved with a group of Marxist intellectuals. He visited the Soviet Union in 1933 as an academic and developed a profound empathy for the communists' ideology. He met like-minded individuals Guy Burgess, Kim Philby, Donald Maclean and John Cairncross at Cambridge. All five went on to work either for the civil service or the intelligence services during the Second World War and all of them passed top secret information to the Soviet Union. They were later to become infamous as "The Cambridge Five".

In 1945 Blunt was appointed Surveyor of the King's Pictures and became Surveyor of the Queen's Pictures after the death of George VI in 1952. By then he was already under suspicion by the security services. Burgess and Maclean had fled to Moscow while under investigation in 1951 and Blunt was questioned as one of their known associates. In 1952 Cairncross admitted to spying, but he escaped prosecution. Philby headed for Moscow in 1963 when it became clear that charges would be brought against him, and when interviewed in 1964 Blunt finally confessed, the evidence against him proving irrefutable. In return for the information he provided, Blunt was given immunity from prosecution.

Having been knighted by the Queen in 1956, Sir Anthony Blunt continued in his role as Surveyor of the Queen's Pictures until 1973, including overseeing the Queen's Gallery at Buckingham Palace, which had opened to the public in 1962. He also continued to expand his career as an art historian, but when pressure from investigative journalists led to Mrs Thatcher making his treachery public knowledge, Blunt was stripped of his knighthood and withdrew from public life, seldom leaving his London home. The palace spy died of a heart attack at the age of 75 in 1983.

CHAPTER EIGHT

THE NEW

ROYAL FAMILY

Having become one of the most photographed women in the world, the Queen came to share her celebrity in the 1980s with two powerful female figures. One was a year older than herself, her first female prime minister, Margaret Thatcher; the other was 35 years younger, her daughter-in-law, Diana, Princess of Wales. The Queen has never sought to dominate the headlines but continues with her work as monarch, diligent and steadfast, shunning publicity save for when it is part of her job. Mrs Thatcher and Princess Diana, however, lived the entire decade in the full glare of media attention – for entirely different reasons.

Mrs Thatcher was at the heart of practically every hard news story from the time of her election in May 1979, through riots, industrial unrest, terrorist attacks, the Falklands War, record economic growth, two further election victories and the build-up to the 1990 Gulf War. For Mrs Thatcher, grabbing the headlines was integral to consolidating her position of power.

Princess Diana, on the other hand, achieved overnight fame as the girl that Britain's future king was to marry. From being a shy, introverted young woman working as a nursery assistant, she became a style and fashion icon, star of a lavish wedding, the face that every tabloid newspaper and magazine editor wanted on the front pages, and mother of the second and third in line to the throne – the new royal family. For Princess Diana, being in the spotlight was at first a shock, then amazingly flattering, then it developed into a part of everyday life that she had to learn to cope with. Ultimately, she would learn not only how to cope with the media, but how to exploit her celebrity.

Far away from Mrs Thatcher's Palace of Westminster and Princess Diana's Kensington Palace, events in the wider world became instant news items through satellite communications technology. The whole world watched as Polish shipyard worker Lech Walesa established the first free trade union in the communist-dominated countries behind the Iron Curtain in September 1980. Soviet leader Mikhail Gorbachev's *glasnost* and *perestroika* initiatives would later lead to a defrosting of the Cold War and the fall of the Berlin Wall in 1989, although the more relaxed relationship with the West was not helped by the secrecy surrounding a devastating explosion at the Soviet Union's Chernobyl nuclear reactor in April 1986. The accident spread radioactive fallout over much of Western Europe.

Throughout the 1980s, there was turmoil in the Middle East, most notably in a prolonged war between Iraq and Iran that cost the lives of hundreds of thousands of combatants and civilians. It was a war that, sadly, was to perpetrate even more conflict in the region

THE LUCKIEST WOMAN ALIVE

In June 1981 the Queen was taking part in the Trooping the Colour ceremony, which is held on the second Saturday of the month in celebration of the sovereign's birthday. It is an event that the Queen has known her whole life and in which she first participated with her father in 1947. The Mall thronged with spectators, held back by crush barriers and lines of police officers and guardsmen, all standing rigidly to attention. The Queen was riding her mare, Burmese, and wearing the scarlet uniform of the Welsh Guards. Riding side-saddle on Burmese at the head of a mounted procession, she was highly visible in the summer sunshine. She could not have made a better target. It was then that the shots were fired. Lance Corporal Galloway of the Scots Guards turned to see a man pointing a revolver at the Queen. He grabbed the man by the hair and dragged him across the barrier, where the gunman was subdued and disarmed.

The Queen continued down The Mall, leaning forwards slightly to give Burmese a reassuring pat. The horse had been slightly spooked – not by the shots but by the way that other riders had suddenly closed in on the Queen to shield her. The procession then continued as normal and the ceremony suffered no further interruptions.

The gunman was 17-year-old Marcus Sarjeant, who had decided to assassinate the Queen in order to become "the most famous teenager in the world". Fortunately, he had been unable to get his hands on a real firearm and was using a blank-firing replica. With the world still reeling from the shootings of US President Ronald Reagan in March and Pope John Paul II in May, the incident gave real cause for concern. Police officers now face out to observe the crowd at such events, rather than in toward the procession, but there were still questions to be asked about the Queen's security.

The previous month, the Queen had been the target of an IRA assassination attempt when she visited the Shetland Islands in the far north of Scotland to open a new oil terminal at Sullom Voe. The facility had been one of Europe's largest construction projects, costing £1.2 billion and employing more than 6,000 workers. One of those workers was secretly a member of the Provisional IRA. He planted a bomb that failed to detonate correctly when it exploded. In fact, the noise that it made scarcely drowned out the band that was playing and most people at the event didn't even notice. The Queen had had another lucky escape – and her luck was to hold when she visited New Zealand later that year.

On 14 October 1981 the Queen was in New Zealand, paying a brief visit following the Commonwealth Heads of Government meeting.

She was attending an event at the Otago Museum Reserve in Dunedin and had just stepped out of her car to talk to assembled well-wishers when what sounded like a shot rang out. At the time, it was dismissed as the noise of a council sign falling over but it was later revealed that a 17-year-old named Christopher Lewis, aiming from an adjacent building, had fired a rifle shot at the Queen. It was sheer good fortune that he missed.

The following year, on 9 July 1982, the Queen awoke in bed at Buckingham Palace at around 7.15 a.m. to find a strange man in her bedroom. It was not unusual for the Queen and Prince Philip to sleep in different bedrooms because they so often had engagements that meant very early starts or staying away overnight. The Queen was alone with the intruder, Michael Fagan, who sat on the edge of her bed and chatted to her about his personal and family problems. The Queen pressed an alarm button by her bed that connected to the police control room in the palace. Nothing happened. She had an opportunity to try another alarm, but again there was no immediate response.

It transpired that the police officer who had been on duty outside her room overnight had finished his shift at 6 a.m. A footman was to replace him temporarily until the next police shift arrived, but the footman was walking the Queen's corgis in the garden. The police control room had initially ignored the alarms because they were notorious for triggering themselves accidentally.

The Queen's ordeal was even more disturbing because Fagan had cut his hand, was bleeding and was holding part of a broken glass ashtray. Having scaled the palace perimeter wall and climbed up a drainpipe to enter through an unlocked window in the roof, he had smashed the ashtray while wandering around the building. According to him, he had broken into the palace before, but it was the first time that he had made it to the Queen's private apartments. He asked for a cigarette and she told him that she would fetch some. She opened her door just as a maid appeared, followed by the footman. He grabbed hold of Fagan and police officers were then swiftly on the scene.

Margaret Thatcher: The Iron Lady

Margaret Thatcher was the longest-serving British prime minister of the modern era, winning three General Elections in a row, two with landslide victories. Her tough stance on both domestic and foreign affairs was divisive, making her the leader that many at home and abroad most loved to hate, and it was the media in the Soviet Union who nicknamed her "The Iron Lady", three years before she became prime minister.

Born Margaret Hilda Roberts on 13 October 1925 in Grantham, Lincolnshire, she was the daughter of Beatrice and Alfred Roberts. Her father was a local grocer and the mayor of Grantham. Margaret won a grammar school scholarship and went on to study chemistry at Oxford. She began to take an active interest in politics at university and later, while working in industry as a research chemist, decided to become an MP. It was through her association with the Conservative Party that she met and married Denis Thatcher in 1951. The couple were to have two children, twins Carol and Mark, who were born in 1953.

Having qualified as a barrister in 1953, Mrs Thatcher did not stand as a candidate in the 1955 General Election because she felt that her young twins needed their mother. In 1959 she was elected MP for Finchley and in 1970 she became Secretary of State for Education and Science in Edward Heath's government. She defeated Heath in the Conservative Party leadership election in 1975 and became Britain's first female prime minister when the Conservatives swept to power in 1979.

Mrs Thatcher came in for heavy criticism as she fought to reduce the power of the trades unions and to privatize state-owned companies. Her autocratic attitude reduced her popularity with the general public but a recovering economy and the 1982 victory in the Falklands War brought her re-election in 1983 and, as Britain began to prosper, she won a third term in 1987. Political infighting led to her resignation in November 1990 and she was given a life peerage as Baroness Thatcher on retiring from the Commons in 1992. Mrs Thatcher suffered from dementia in her later years and died in 2013 aged 87.

Much has been made of Mrs Thatcher's relationship with the Queen, with some suggesting that they did not like each other. Those close to both women maintain that each had a great deal of respect for the other, and in her 1993 memoir *The Downing Street Years*, Mrs Thatcher wrote that "stories of clashes between two powerful women were just too good not to make up".

THE FALKLANDS WAR

The Queen was not the only member of her immediate family who found herself in dangerous situations during the early 1980s. Prince Andrew was to become the first British royal to see active service in a combat zone since his father had done so during the Second World War. Having joined the Royal Navy in 1979, the prince had trained as a helicopter pilot, earned his pilot's "wings" and gone on to advanced training, qualifying as a Sea King pilot. In 1982 he was assigned to 820 Naval Air Squadron aboard the aircraft carrier HMS *Invincible*. Then, on 2 April 1982, Argentina invaded the Falkland Islands.

The Falkland Islands, South Georgia and the South Sandwich Islands were British dependencies in the South Atlantic populated by British citizens. Sovereignty of the islands had been in dispute ever since the first settlers inhabited the islands in 1764, but they had been firmly in British hands since 1833. Argentina, however, continued to lay claim to the territories, with a romantic myth developing in the country that they rightfully belonged to Argentina. As a way of deflecting attention from the poor state of the economy and the unpopularity of the ruling military regime, the Argentine government decided to seize the islands by landing troops.

Defended by only a small detachment of Royal Marines, who were ordered to surrender after putting up a brave show of defiance, the islands were soon under the control of Argentine forces. They had assumed that Britain, 8,000 miles (12,875 kilometres) away and barely able to maintain its military commitments – there had been constant reports of defence cutbacks – would not be able to mount a credible counter-attack. They were wrong. The day before the invasion, when Argentine intentions became clear, Royal Navy ships on exercise in the Mediterranean were ordered to prepare to sail south. Other elements of the task force, including nuclear-powered submarines, were already on their way to the Falklands before the first troops of the main Argentine invasion force had even landed.

Three days after the invasion, HMS *Invincible* left Portsmouth headed for the South Atlantic with Prince Andrew on board. The Admiralty had wanted to assign the prince to a UK-based administrative role during the conflict, but he was insistent that he should be allowed to serve alongside his shipmates. The Queen agreed and, as commander-in-chief of Britain's armed forces, she was not to be argued with. Prince Andrew had a difficult and dangerous job flying the Sea King. It was the largest of the Royal Navy's helicopters and a true workhorse, with the prince flying anti-submarine patrols, casualty evacuation flights and flying as a decoy for Argentina's Exocet missiles. Being a decoy entailed hovering near the stern of HMS *Invincible* where the Sea King would present a large radar target – in theory this would distract the on-board radar of the missile, fooling it into targeting the Sea King instead of the carrier. The helicopter pilot then had to dodge the missile by climbing rapidly and allowing the missile, supposedly programmed not to fly above a certain height, to pass safely underneath. The prince later described to journalists how disconcerting it was to have the targeting radar of his own ship's anti-aircraft missiles lock onto his Sea King, something that happened three times. "It really makes the hair stand up on the back of your neck," he said. "It is not much fun having one of those fellows pick you out as a target."

The task force assembled by the British military included the ocean liners *Canberra* and *Queen Elizabeth II*, requisitioned to act as troop carriers, along with 125 other ships. Although some authorities, including the US Navy, did not believe it was possible to retake the Falklands without a forward operating base and air superiority, plans were finalized as the task force sailed south. The war was to last for 74 days, costing the lives of 649 Argentine personnel, 255 British personnel and three Falkland Islanders. The Argentines surrendered when Port Stanley, the islands' capital, was retaken on 14 June 1982.

VIOLENT BRITAIN

Throughout the 1980s, in the poorest areas of cities across the country, especially Bristol, Leeds, Liverpool and London, disaffected black and Asian groups protested about sub-standard housing, high rates of unemployment within their communities and the new "stop-and-search" laws that the police appeared to be applying disproportionately to young black and Asian men. The protests often turned violent as the protestors clashed with police and predominantly white counter-demonstrators from the right-wing National Front. These "race riots" featured heavily on television news, showing images of running battles in the streets, vehicles set ablaze and business premises ransacked.

While the riots flared up in particular hotspots from time to time, the IRA seemed determined to demonstrate that they could strike almost anywhere on mainland Britain, whenever they chose. They detonated bombs outside Chelsea Barracks in London, a burger bar on Oxford Street in London and the Royal Marines School of Music in Deal, Kent, each time claiming lives and causing horrific injuries. On 20 July 1982, at 10.40 a.m., a car bomb was detonated in Hyde Park, London, as members of the Household Cavalry rode past during the daily Changing of the Guard procession. Four soldiers died and many more were wounded. Seven horses were also killed. A little over two hours later an IRA bomb destroyed the bandstand in Regent's Park, London, where the band of the Royal Green Jackets had been playing to a crowd of 120 people. Seven bandsmen died and many more were wounded, including at least eight of their civilian audience.

The IRA's most high-profile attack came on 12 October 1984 in Brighton when they blew up the Grand Hotel, where the Conservative Party leadership, including Prime Minister Margaret Thatcher, were staying during their annual party conference. Mrs Thatcher escaped injury but five people died and 31 were badly injured. One of those who died was a Conservative MP, Sir Anthony Berry. The attack happened at 2.54 a.m., yet the party conference opened as usual the following day at 9.30 a.m. with the prime minister proclaiming that "...this attack has failed... all attempts to destroy democracy by terrorism will fail".

Mrs Thatcher took a similarly tough stance when dealing with industrial unrest. Striking miners came into conflict with the police and non-striking miners in a series of increasingly violent clashes. In April a miner died after being hit on the head when stones were thrown at Ollerton in Nottinghamshire and two months later another was killed when trying to stop a truck delivering coal to a power station in West Yorkshire. Then, on 18 June 1984, 5,000 pickets from all over the UK assembled outside a facility in Orgreave, South Yorkshire. They were confronted by 6,000 police officers, some equipped with riot gear, 42 of them mounted on police horses. In what became known as "The Battle of Orgreave", the miners fought with police, the mounted police charged the crowd, and shocking scenes of violence were screened on television news broadcasts. Almost 100 arrests were made and 51 striking miners were injured, as were 72 police officers.

ROYAL WEDDINGS AND ROYAL GRANDCHILDREN

In the early 1980s Prince Charles came under increasing pressure to find himself a bride. He had been associated with a number of young ladies in the past including, during the early 1970s, Camilla Shand, but in 1980 speculation became rife that he was courting the 19-year-old Lady Diana Spencer. Lady Diana had quite close connections to the royal family through her father, who had been equerry to both King George VI and Queen Elizabeth II. Her grandmother, Lady Fermoy, had been lady-in-waiting to the Queen Mother. Lady Diana was, therefore, well known to the royal family.

Diana had been born on the Sandringham estate on 1 July 1961 and was educated at private schools, including West Heath Girls' School – a boarding school in Kent that boasted only 100 pupils, including Diana's sisters Sarah and Jane. She spent some time at a finishing school in Switzerland before her mother – her parents had divorced when she was seven – gave her a flat in London's Earl's Court as an 18th birthday present. When the news broke of her romance with Prince Charles, Diana was working as a nursery assistant and was catapulted, almost overnight, from being a little-known young woman enjoying her lifestyle in London into becoming the most photographed woman in the world.

Hungry for news that would assuage the everyday monotony of political quarrels and industrial unrest, the press clamoured to print photos of the prince's pretty new girlfriend on their front pages. When their engagement was announced on 24 February 1981, the news cut through the winter gloom like a ray of sunshine.

The day of the wedding was to be 29 July 1981. By that date Diana would be just 20 years old. Planning the event in only five months was a mammoth task. The venue was St Paul's Cathedral, chosen partly because it could hold more guests than Westminster Abbey, and the bride left from Clarence House (where she had been living since the announcement of the engagement) accompanied by her father, John Spencer, 8th Earl Spencer. They rode in a horse-drawn glass carriage with large glass windows and gold-liveried coachmen, accompanied by mounted Metropolitan Police officers. The royal family left from Buckingham Palace, riding in a series of open coaches with Prince Charles accompanied by his supporter, Prince Andrew. He had two supporters, his brothers Andrew and Edward, rather than a best man. Prince Edward rode with his sister, Princess Anne.

When Diana arrived at St Paul's the world got its first glimpse of the best-kept secret of 1981: the royal wedding dress. Looking slightly crumpled after having been squashed into the carriage, the dress was shimmering silk embroidered with 10,000 mother-of-pearl sequins and pearls. The train stretched to 25 feet (7.6 metres) and Diana had gone through special rehearsals to learn how to walk while dragging the train behind her.

There were 3,500 guests in St Paul's for the ceremony but an estimated two million on the processional route, cheering and singing in the summer sunshine. During the ceremony, there was near-silence on the street as the crowds congregated around transistor radios to listen. There were no mobile phones or other devices capable of instant streaming at that time, although the service was broadcast live on television to a worldwide audience believed to be around 750 million.

With all of the gleaming uniforms, glamour and theatricality of the greatest of royal occasions, the event had certainly lived up to its billing as a "fairytale wedding" by the time the prince emerged from St Paul's with his beautiful princess on his arm. Sadly, this fairytale was not to have a happy ending.

Five years later, on 23 July 1986, Prince Andrew married Sarah Ferguson at Westminster Abbey. The second royal wedding of the decade was never going to compete with that of Charles and Diana, now Prince and Princess of Wales, but the streets were nevertheless lined once again with well-wishers. Prior to the ceremony, the Queen had created Prince Andrew Duke of York, the title traditionally held by the sovereign's second son – the title her father had held when she was born. After the ceremony the new Duke and Duchess of York appeared on the balcony at Buckingham Palace with a crowd estimated at 100,000 outside the gates. They playfully pretended not to hear when the crowd roared for the royal couple to kiss – this departure from royal tradition was not something that Prince Andrew's parents would ever have done, but it was one that had been pioneered by his elder brother. They then obliged with what is now very much a traditional "balcony kiss".

With three of the Queen's children now married, Buckingham Palace was once again to experience children romping through its corridors. The first of the royal grandchildren was Peter Phillips, born to Princess Anne and (by then) Captain Mark Phillips on 15 November 1977. Unlike other royal husbands, such as Earl Snowdon, it is believed that Captain Phillips declined a peerage, so his two children with Princess Anne – Zara Phillips came along in 1981 – have no courtesy titles.

Prince William became second in line to the throne when he was born to the Prince and Princess of Wales on 21 June 1982, and the couple had another child, Prince Harry, on 15 September 1984. Four years later, the Duke and Duchess of York had their first daughter, Princess Beatrice, born on 8 August 1988. Her sister, Princess Eugenie, was born on 23 March 1990. The Queen's family was growing but it was soon to become clear that the new royal family was far from a happy one.

CHAPTER NINE

THE QUEEN'S
DARKEST DAYS

The British economy had been climbing steadily uphill during the later Thatcher years with rising wages, rising house prices and a boom in the stock market. By the early 1990s, however, with John Major as Prime Minister, the country was on a downward trajectory, leading to a recession in 1991–92. The low point came on Black Wednesday, 16 September 1992, when the pound fell in value to such an extent that Britain was forced to withdraw from the European Exchange Rate Mechanism (ERM), the system established within the European Economic Community (EEC) to help stabilize the currencies of member states. This was especially embarrassing because Britain held the presidency of the EEC at the time.

A steady recovery was to ensue, with unemployment and inflation figures falling, but John Major's Conservative government was beset by other problems, rocked by sex scandals and financial philandering that paved the way for the Labour Party landslide victory in the 1997 election. The Queen's 10th prime minister was Tony Blair who set the ball rolling for the United Kingdom to become a little less united.

Referendums in 1997 paved the way for a Scottish Parliament and Welsh Assembly in 1999.

Abroad, the UK sovereign territory of Hong Kong was reclaimed by China and the Prince of Wales attended the handover ceremony on 1 July 1997. When he left Victoria Harbour on board HMY *Britannia* it marked the moment when the days of empire were well and truly over. The same could be said of the USSR with Soviet leader Mikhail Gorbachev having resigned, dissolving the union on 25 December 1991. He handed power in Moscow to the President of Russia Boris Yeltsin after the Soviet states had, one by one, declared themselves independent republics. The rise of nationalism saw the former communist federal state of Yugoslavia split into its constituent republics. Thousands were to die there in bitter fighting and ethnic massacres.

In the Middle East, Iraq, desperate to recoup its losses after a crippling war with Iran, invaded Kuwait in August 1990. President Saddam Hussein's battle-hardened troops quickly overran the smaller, oil-rich Kuwait and were soon at the border with Saudi Arabia. To protect the Saudi oil fields and to expel Saddam Hussein from Kuwait, a military coalition of more than 30 nations, led by the USA, launched Operation Desert Storm on 17 January 1991. The Iraqis were driven back to their own border by 28 February.

Amid all of this turmoil, the Queen, having seen the joys of weddings and christenings in the 1980s, was about to suffer the darkest days of her reign.

THE *"ANNUS HORRIBILIS"*

The 1990s had barely begun when the Queen was to experience one year, 1992, that she would famously describe as her *"annus horribilis"*. Although the Queen was no stranger to family controversy, she was overwhelmed by personal turmoils early in the decade that would have floored most grandmothers in their mid-70s. Previously, her greatest source of consternation had been her sister, Princess Margaret, who, rather than settling down after her marriage to Lord Snowdon, had continued to make herself an easy target for the tabloid press. The couple's marriage appeared to become quite an open arrangement and the media were quick to pick up on potential relationships between the princess and men other than her husband. In 1976 the couple announced that their marriage had broken down and they were divorced in 1978. It was the first time that a senior member of the royal family had divorced in more than 70 years. Sadly, it was not to be the last.

During the 1980s Princess Anne and her husband Captain Mark Phillips had grown apart to the extent that he fathered a child by another woman in 1985. In 1989 intimate letters to Princess Anne were stolen from Buckingham Palace and offered to a tabloid newspaper. The letters were from one of the Queen's equerries, Commander Timothy Laurence. Once again, the tortured love lives of the royals became the subject of public speculation and it was announced that the princess and her husband were to separate.

These sad, headline-grabbing stories were, however, simply a prelude to the tortuous events of 1992. The press had latched on to the fact that the Duchess of York was increasingly being seen in the company of other men while Prince Andrew was away either with the Royal Navy or on royal engagements. It became clear that their marriage was in trouble and on 19 March 1992 they announced their separation, although they remained on good terms. They divorced on 30 May 1992, only a month after the divorce of Princess Anne.

In August 1992 the latest in a series of photographs of the Duchess of York sunbathing in the company of a Texan businessman appeared on the front page of the *Daily Mirror* newspaper. The photographs showed him kissing her feet and it was clear that she was topless, with the princesses Beatrice and Eugenie close by. Embarrassingly, the duchess was with the royal family at Balmoral when the photographs appeared.

Just a few days later the *Sun* newspaper published transcripts of a phone call between Diana, Princess of Wales, and a long-time friend James Gilbey, during which Diana made scathing comments about the royal family. It had already become clear that the Wales's marriage was in trouble when journalist Andrew Morton's book *Diana: Her True Story* had been published in June and serialized beforehand in the *Sunday*

Times. The book had been written with the co-operation of the princess and revealed details of her struggle with bulimia, her suicide attempts and how she had turned to others for affection when it became obvious to her that her husband had resumed his relationship with his old girlfriend Camilla Shand, who was by then Camilla Parker Bowles.

Then, on Friday 20 November 1992 – the day that the Queen and Prince Philip celebrated their 45th wedding anniversary – a fire broke out at Windsor Castle. It began in the Queen's Private Chapel at 11.15 a.m. when a curtain was set on fire by the heat from a spotlight that was too close. A fire alarm sounded in the watch room of the castle fire brigade but members of the royal household were already on the scene, having spotted the burning curtain, and immediately started to remove works of art from the chapel. The fire spread very quickly, even though the castle fire crew, based two miles away, was on the scene in minutes. Workmen who had been carrying out renovations used fire extinguishers to try to help douse the flames. Prince Andrew had been working in the royal archives at the time and helped staff to remove paintings and furniture from rooms that appeared to be in the path of the blaze. He also telephoned the Queen to let her know what was happening.

The fire spread through the roof void at an alarming rate and soon a substantial part of the state apartments was ablaze. Fire crews rushed to the castle and there were ultimately more than 35 fire appliances on the scene manned by over 200 firefighters. Flames reached 50 feet (15 metres) high, ceilings and roofs collapsed, and at one time there were fears for three missing firefighters. Lost in dense smoke, they were safely located but it took almost nine hours to bring the blaze under control. The last of the flames were eventually doused 15 hours after the alarm had been raised. Nine state apartments and 100 other rooms were destroyed but a rescue operation staged by military personnel, staff from Windsor Castle and the estate, building contractors and others – hundreds of willing hands – had saved valuable carpets, manuscripts, paintings, chandeliers, clocks, porcelain, books and items of furniture. There were no serious injuries.

The Queen had been in London when she was told of the fire and rushed immediately to Windsor, watching the salvage operation and the firefighters battle to bring the blaze under control. This was the place where she had grown up, a home that she had known all of her life, and she was clearly distressed at the scale of the inferno. She returned the following morning to inspect the damage. The private apartments where she and her family lived had survived unscathed yet the destruction of so much of the place that she so adored was devastating.

The Queen summed up her feelings about 1992 in a speech at Guildhall, where she attended an official lunch to commemorate the 40th anniversary of her succession. She borrowed a phrase from a former equerry Sir Edward Ford, who had written to express his hope that her 40th as sovereign would be an *annus mirabilis* ("wonderful year") but that it had instead become an *annus horribilis* ("horrible year").

> 1992 is not a year on which I shall look back with undiluted pleasure. In the words of one of my more sympathetic correspondents, it has turned out to be an annus horribilis. I suspect that I am not alone in thinking it so...
>
> ...I sometimes wonder how future generations will judge the events of this tumultuous year. I dare say that history will take a slightly more moderate view than that of some contemporary commentators.

The Queen was suffering from a cold and her voice had been further affected by the smoke at Windsor, making her sound more emotional than her usual delivery. In an effort to ensure that she would not lose her voice, the Queen gave the speech before rather than after lunch. While the speech made reference to the way that some "commentators" in the media had treated the royal family, she also thanked her host, the Lord Mayor of London, for "the loyalty given to me and to my family by so many people in this country and the Commonwealth throughout my reign". The royal family was to need all of that support in the years to come. Less than a month after her speech, on 9 December, Prime Minister John Major announced in the House of Commons that the Prince and Princess of Wales were to separate.

Tony Blair: Icon of New Labour

At 43 years of age Tony Blair became the youngest British prime minister for 185 years when his "New Labour" party swept to power with a landslide victory in the 1997 General Election. He brought 18 years of Conservative rule to an end and initiated 13 years of Labour government – the longest continuous period that Labour has ever remained in power.

Although born in Edinburgh on 6 May 1953, Anthony Charles Lynton Blair's family moved to Australia when he was less than two years old. His father was a law lecturer at Adelaide University for four years, after which the Blairs moved back to Scotland. His father then lectured at Durham, where Blair spent most of his childhood. He went to Fettes College in Edinburgh aged 13, and by the age of 18 he was in London, attempting to become involved in the rock music business. He eventually studied law at Oxford University, where he developed an interest in politics.

Blair studied to become a barrister in London, where he met the woman who was to become his wife, Cherie Booth. Having joined the Labour Party in 1975, Blair stood for election unsuccessfully a couple of times before becoming MP for Sedgefield in County Durham in 1983. He became leader of the Labour Party in 1994, promoting a change in approach. The Labour Party had already been moving slowly away from the far left but Blair made the shift seem like a giant leap.

In the 1997 General Election the British public gave Blair's "New Labour" their endorsement, returning 418 Labour MPs, the most the party had ever had. It was the Conservative Party's worst defeat in over 90 years. The Blairs moved into Downing Street with their three children, occupying the flat at No. 11, traditionally the Chancellor of the Exchequer's residence, rather than the one at No. 10 because No. 11 has more space. Their fourth child, Leo, was born in 2000, the first child born to a serving prime minister and his wife in 150 years.

Tony Blair's premiership was notable for the Bank of England becoming independent; the huge steps toward peace in Northern Ireland with the signing of the Good Friday Agreement and the IRA decommissioning its weapons; devolution, with the establishment of the Welsh Assembly and Scottish Parliament; and employment reforms, including the National Minimum Wage. He also agreed to support the USA in the 2001 invasion of Afghanistan and the 2003 invasion of Iraq.

Blair remains the only Labour leader to have won three General Elections in a row, but Labour had a vastly reduced majority in the 2005 election and the war in Iraq had decimated Blair's personal popularity ratings. He resigned in 2007.

"THE WAR OF THE WALESES"

Windsor Castle is not merely a royal residence. It is not a private home, although the royal family has private apartments within the castle. It is, in fact, the largest inhabited castle in the world, with over 200 people living and working within its walls. It is also the world's oldest continuously occupied castle, with a fortification having stood on the site for around 1,000 years. It is a major tourist attraction but it was not insured – the cost of any "house and contents" insurance policy would not only have been prohibitive but also almost impossible to calculate. The repair and restoration costs were estimated at £37 million.

Because Windsor Castle is a state asset it seemed obvious that the government should fund the restoration work, but it was decided that the money should come from the privy purse, which is the Queen's private income. A trust was set up to accept private donations toward the restoration and other funding was to come from fees charged for entry to certain areas of the castle and from entry fees to Buckingham Palace, which began opening to the public during the summer from 1993 onwards. The Queen contributed £2 million of her own money. Prince Philip was heavily involved in overseeing the restoration, which entailed craftsmen reviving and relearning some traditional masonry skills and woodworking techniques. Rebuilding, recreating ornate plaster ceilings, painting, gilding and restoration went on for five years. The work finished in 1997, ahead of time and below budget.

On 14 November 1997 the Queen and Prince Philip held a reception in the refurbished rooms for 1,500 people who had worked on the restoration of Windsor Castle. A week later they held a ball there to celebrate their Golden Wedding anniversary. The celebrations also included a garden party at Buckingham Palace with couples from all over the country who were also celebrating their 50th wedding anniversaries in the same year as the Queen, a thanksgiving service at Westminster Abbey, a reception with Prime Minister Tony Blair at 10 Downing Street and a lunch at Guildhall in London where the Queen gave a speech paying tribute to her husband:

He is someone who doesn't take easily to compliments but has, quite simply, been my strength and stay all these years and I, and his whole family, and this and many other countries, owe him a debt greater than he would ever claim or we shall ever know.

The Queen's confidence in the strength of her marriage was not reflected in the state of her eldest son's relationship with his wife. In fact, the increasingly antagonistic situation between the Prince and Princess of Wales was to be dubbed by the media as "The War of the Waleses".

In January 1993 transcripts of an intimate, late-night telephone conversation between the prince and Camilla Parker Bowles were published in the press. Quite how this recording, and the earlier recording of Diana talking to James Gilbey, had been made and how they found their way into the hands of the tabloids is still the subject of huge speculation but the damage that they did was undeniable.

The final official trips that Prince Charles and Princess Diana took together were visits to India and South Korea in 1992. In India photographs of Diana sitting alone in front of the Taj Mahal made the front pages, seeming to symbolize her deteriorating marriage. That was almost certainly the effect for which the princess had been aiming when she posed for the pictures. The press had hounded her during the previous decade to the extent that the Queen called a meeting of senior reporters and editors at Buckingham Palace to persuade them to take a less-intrusive approach. It had little effect, but by now Princess Diana was far more confident in dealing with the press. She had hired a voice coach to improve her public speaking and she was in great demand, associated with over 100 charities. Yet, in December 1993 she announced that she was to withdraw from public life, saying:

Over the next few months I will be seeking a more suitable way of combining a meaningful public role with, hopefully, a more private life. My first priority will continue to be our children, William and Harry, who deserve as much love, and care, and attention as I am able to give…

The princess was never far from the news but taking time out gave her the chance to manage her public persona more effectively. When Prince Charles worked with author and broadcaster David Dimbleby on a 1994 book and television documentary about his life and work, he admitted his infidelity with Camilla Parker Bowles, claiming that he had remained faithful to his wife until his marriage broke down. Princess Diana countered with revelations about her marriage in videotapes that had been made during her voice coaching sessions and, in 1995, with an interview for the BBC's *Panorama* current affairs programme. Referring to Camilla Parker Bowles, she told journalist Martin Bashir that "...there were three of us in this marriage, so it was a bit crowded". She also cast doubts over Prince Charles's suitability to be king and admitted that, although she would never be queen, she would like to be thought of as "a queen of people's hearts".

The situation had now become unbearable for the Queen and she wrote to her son and his wife telling them that they should divorce. The divorce was finalized on 15 July 1996. Just over a year later, on 31 August 1997, Diana, Princess of Wales, was dead. A car in which she was a passenger crashed in a tunnel in Paris while trying to evade press photographers. The driver and the man with whom Diana had been romantically linked, Dodi Al-Fayed, were also killed and the only other passenger, Diana's bodyguard Trevor Rees-Jones, was seriously injured.

The nation mourned Diana and questions were asked of the royal family, who were at Balmoral when the tragedy happened. The Queen was criticized for not rushing down to London to share the public grief and it was even pointed out that the royal standard was not flying at half mast over Buckingham Palace. In fact, the royal standard is only flown when the sovereign is actually in residence at the palace. The Queen had seen her main duty as being to her grandchildren, Prince William and Prince Harry, who were with her at Balmoral. She and Prince Philip arrived in London on 5 September and were applauded by the thousands who gathered each day to add to the mountain of floral tributes piled against the railings of Buckingham Palace and Princess Diana's residence at Kensington Palace.

Bill Clinton: A Most Popular President

Only two US presidents have ever been impeached, the process through which the House of Representatives can bring charges of "high crimes and misdemeanours" against high-ranking public servants. The first was President Andrew Johnson, whose alleged crime was an administrative transgression in 1868. After being impeached, the accused faces a trial in the United States Senate where senators vote on whether the charges have been proved and the accused should be removed from office. A two-thirds majority is required. Johnson was acquitted.

President Richard Nixon, whom many might think was impeached over the famous "Watergate" scandal, actually resigned in 1974 before any impeachment proceedings could be brought against him. The second president to be impeached was actually Bill Clinton in 1998. He was faced with charges of perjury and obstruction of justice relating to the testimony he gave to a Grand Jury about allegations of sexual misconduct with White House intern Monica Lewinsky. President Clinton was also acquitted.

Born William Jefferson Blythe III on 19 August 1946 in Hope, Arkansas, Bill Clinton's father was travelling salesman William Jefferson Blythe Jr., who died three months before his son was born. His mother was Virginia Dell Cassidy, but it transpired that Blythe had

The Queen made a live broadcast from Buckingham Palace, with the crowds of mourners at the palace gates in the background. She paid tribute to the princess, saying that, "...I admired and respected her for her energy and commitment to others and especially for her devotion to her two boys. This week at Balmoral we have all been trying to help William and Harry come to terms with the devastating loss that they and the rest of us have suffered."

On 6 September there was a full state funeral for the princess. Prince William and Prince Harry, aged 15 and 12, walked behind the coffin, through streets lined with people, all the way to Westminster Abbey. Prince Charles, Prince Philip and Diana's brother accompanied still been married to a previous wife when he had married Cassidy, making the marriage bigamous. Clinton's mother later married car dealer Roger Clinton Sr., whose name Bill took when he was 15.

At school, Clinton became involved in student politics and was a talented saxophone player. He studied at Georgetown University in Washington, DC, and won a prestigious Rhodes Scholarship to Oxford University, where he studied politics, before returning to the USA to study law at Yale. It was there that he met Hillary Rodham and they married in 1975. They had one daughter, Chelsea.

Clinton worked as a Law Professor at the University of Arkansas before becoming Arkansas Attorney General in 1976 and Governor of Arkansas in 1978. He lost an election two years later but was re-elected as Governor in 1982, remaining in office for 10 years. He was inaugurated as President of the USA in January 1993.

President Clinton raised taxes rather than lowering them as he had promised during his election campaign and over the course of his presidency he introduced reforms to welfare and child healthcare, and he reduced the burden of legislation on financial institutions. His last three years in office saw budget surpluses, a situation that had not occurred for 30 years and helped to make him popular. Opinion polls conducted by the Gallup organization during his final months in office gave him a higher public approval rating than any president in 50 years.

them. More than 32 million viewers in the UK watched the funeral on television. Millions more watched around the world.

Some thought that the circumstances surrounding the death of Princess Diana and the problems that had dogged the royal family throughout the 1990s might spell the beginning of the end for the monarchy in Britain. Nothing could have been further from the truth.

T H E   N E W

G E N E R A T I O N

In the Queen's 2017 Christmas broadcast, she referred to how technology had changed since her first televised Christmas message in 1957, saying, "...who could have imagined that people would one day be watching this on laptops and mobile phones...". Sixty years of communications advances, bringing us 24-hour newsfeeds, the Internet and "social media" have made it possible for pretty much anyone to become an instant broadcaster. Sadly, that has proved not always to be a good thing.

The twenty-first century has seen the inexorable rise of extremist Islamic terrorism and all terrorists are now adept at harnessing technology to spread their message of fear. Images of the attacks on the World Trade Center and the Pentagon on 11 September 2001 flashed around the globe and shocked the world. They led to US President George W. Bush declaring a "War on Terror" and prolonged campaigns in Afghanistan and Iraq. Al Qaeda terror leader Osama Bin Laden became the world's most wanted man and there were murderous attacks by lone wolves or small terror groups in the hearts of cities throughout the free world. Some groups claimed affiliation to Al Qaeda, others to Islamic State, a potent force that had proclaimed a "caliphate" in areas of war-torn Syria and Iraq in 2014.

For the Queen, her work with the Commonwealth in bringing nations together has become more important than ever. The steadfast stability of the royal family is as relevant today as it ever has been. Her family, of course, has seen its share of joy and sadness in the new millennium: the Queen's younger sister, Princess Margaret, died in February 2002 at the age of 71 and the Queen Mother, having received the traditional message of congratulations from her daughter in 2000 that the Queen sends to every centenarian, died only a month after Princess Margaret. The Queen Mother's funeral was a most solemn yet magnificent occasion, with the tenor bell at Westminster Abbey tolling 101 times – once for each year of her life.

As the century progressed there was much to celebrate. In 2012 came the Queen's Diamond Jubilee and in 2016 the Queen reached her 90th year and Prince Philip his 95th. The Queen was also delighted to see the first of her grandchildren marrying, and the arrival of the first of her great-grandchildren. She has certainly been assured by the way that the younger generations of royalty have embraced their duties, making the British royal family more popular than ever and meaning that there is a golden future for the House of Windsor.

THE MILLENNIUM WEDDINGS

Although the 1990s plunged the Queen into more family crises than any mother should ever have to bear, there were also a number of high points, with none more pleasing for her than the marriage of her youngest son, Prince Edward, to Sophie Rhys-Jones on 19 June 1999 – the final royal wedding of the twentieth century.

Edward had himself contributed to the darkest decade of his mother's reign when he had quit the Royal Marines in 1987. Although it is no secret that at least one-third of the officers who take the gruelling commando training course at the Royal Marines base in Lympstone,

Devon, fail through injury or unsuitability, the nation was shocked when the prince dropped out. It appeared that he did so because, being honest with himself, his family and his Royal Marine superiors, he simply did not feel that he was suited to a military career. His commandant, Colonel Ian Moore, said to reporters: "Let me make it quite clear that he was doing well in his training. His instructors, who all had a lot of time for him, respected him. He had all the physical ability to complete his training satisfactorily – indeed well." Other marines were somewhat less charitable when they were seen sporting t-shirts bearing the slogan on the front "You can turn a frog into a prince…" and on the back "But you can't turn a prince into a Royal Marine."

Prince Edward later pursued a career in the entertainment industry, working for a couple of theatre companies, including Andrew Lloyd Webber's Really Useful Theatre Company, before setting up his own company, Ardent Productions. Ardent ceased to exist in 2009, by which time Prince Edward was far more involved in royal duties, easing some of the burden on Prince Philip. While he was playing in a charity "royal tennis" or "real tennis" tournament, an ancient sport that is akin to a cross between tennis and squash, he met PR executive Sophie, who was also playing. The couple kept in close touch and eventually announced their engagement on 6 January 1999.

Prince Edward and Sophie opted for a less-ostentatious wedding ceremony than his two older brothers had had in the 1980s, marrying in Windsor at St George's Chapel. Neither the groom nor his two supporters – his brothers Prince Charles and Prince Andrew – were in uniform. They wore morning suits, although this scarcely detracted from the grandeur of the occasion, with thousands lining the streets in Windsor for the wedding procession and up to 200 million watching on television around the world.

The first royal wedding of the new millennium was that of Prince Charles and his partner, Camilla Parker Bowles, on 9 April 2005. Camilla had previously been married to Brigadier Andrew Parker Bowles, who was a godson of the Queen Mother, had once played on Prince Charles's polo team and had at one time dated Princess Anne. Camilla and her husband had two children, Tom and Laura, but had divorced in 1995, parting on amicable terms. Andrew Parker Bowles married his second wife, Rosemary, a year later and they attended the wedding of Prince Charles and Camilla.

Objections had been raised in some quarters about whether it would be legal for Charles to marry a divorced woman whose previous husband was still alive. The Church of England, as King Edward VIII and Princess Margaret had found to their cost, had previously refused to recognize such a marriage. Following her divorce from Captain Mark Phillips, Princess Anne had married Commander Timothy Laurence at Craithie Kirk near Balmoral in December 1992, one of the few brighter moments in the Queen's *annus horribilis*. The couple chose to marry in Scotland because the Church of Scotland took a more pragmatic view on divorced persons being married in church. The Church of England relaxed its rules in 2002, but there remained some who believed that it might not be appropriate or even legal for Prince Charles, the future head of the Church of England, to marry a divorcee. The government eventually stepped in with a legal ruling to allay any fears that the future king might be about to become involved in a marriage that was in any way improper. The Secretary of State for Constitutional Affairs and Lord Chancellor, Lord Falconer, said in the House of Lords that, "The government are satisfied that it is lawful for the Prince of Wales and Mrs Parker Bowles, like anyone else, to marry by civil ceremony in accordance with Part III of the Marriage Act 1949."

Nevertheless, the Queen and Prince Philip did not attend the civil ceremony at Windsor Guildhall, although they were at the later blessing by the Archbishop of Canterbury in St George's Chapel, Windsor Castle, and hosted a reception for the couple in the castle afterwards. Witnesses at the wedding ceremony were Prince William and Tom Parker Bowles.

The first of the Queen's grandchildren to marry was Peter Phillips. Having studied at Exeter University, Phillips later worked for Jaguar Cars and the Williams Formula One racing team. He met Autumn Kelly, a Canadian management consultant, at the 2003 Canadian Grand Prix in Montreal. The couple married at St George's Chapel in Windsor on 17 May 2008 and spent some time living in Hong Kong, where Phillips worked for the Royal Bank of Scotland.

One of Autumn's bridesmaids was Zara Phillips, her new husband's sister. Like her mother, Zara had made a name for herself as an equestrian. She won individual and team gold medals at the European Eventing Championship in 2005 and went on to become Eventing World Champion. Again like her mother, she became BBC Sports Personality of the Year – Princess Anne won it in 1971 and Zara won it in 2006 – and she represented Great Britain in the Olympic Games. Zara won silver in the team eventing and was presented with her medal by her mother. It was in Australia in 2003 that Prince Harry introduced Zara to England rugby player Mike Tindall, who was in the country playing in England's victorious World Cup squad. The two became an item and Buckingham Palace announced their engagement on 21 December 2010 and they were married at Canongate Kirk on Edinburgh's Royal Mile on 30 July 2011.

The day before the wedding they held a drinks reception aboard the royal yacht *Britannia*, by then permanently moored at Ocean Terminal, Leith, on the Firth of Forth just outside Edinburgh. *Britannia* had been retired following her final voyage, to bring home the last governor of Hong Kong and Prince Charles after the handing back of Hong Kong to the Chinese. Prior to that the ship had completed one of her most famous voyages in October 1994 when she was moored on the Neva, the river on whose banks stands the Russian city of St Petersburg. This was part of the first-ever state visit to Russia by a reigning British monarch. Prior to arriving in St Petersburg, the Queen and Prince Philip had flown to Moscow, where they stayed at the Kremlin, but in St Petersburg they had the comfort and security of *Britannia*. The ship, as always, was prepared and equipped to act as a floating embassy. It delivered the royal Rolls-Royce in which the Queen and her husband toured the city and the Queen hosted a banquet aboard *Britannia* with Russia's President Boris Yeltsin as guest of honour. They dined on the finest salmon and venison from the royal estate at Balmoral, but the Russian president was not impressed, later telling reporters that "Russian food is better".

While Zara's mother and father had enjoyed their honeymoon aboard *Britannia* in the West Indies, her uncle Prince Charles had sailed the Mediterranean aboard the yacht on honeymoon with Princess Diana, and her uncle Prince Andrew had also spent part of his honeymoon with the Duchess of York on *Britannia*, Zara had to settle for a party by the quayside. Although the ship had served the nation and the royal family well ever since the Queen and Prince Philip first boarded her off the coast of Libya in 1954, the cost of refitting her for the twenty-first century was deemed too great and she was decommissioned in 1997 at a ceremony attended by most senior members of the royal family. The Queen was seen to wipe a tear from her eye. Permanently moored at Leith, *Britannia* is now used for private functions and attracts more than 300,000 tourists every year.

WILLIAM AND CATHERINE

No other royal wedding could ever compete with what was billed as the most elaborate, most glamorous marriage ceremony of the modern age when Prince William and Catherine Middleton took their vows in Westminster Abbey on 29 April 2011.

The couple had met while studying at St Andrews University. Their relationship had started when they fell in with the same group of friends, but when their romance developed it did so under the burden of constant press speculation. It was not something that Catherine had ever experienced before, but for Prince William it was an all-too-familiar intrusion.

Catherine was the daughter of Michael and Carole Middleton. Her father worked for British Airways and her mother had been a British Airways flight attendant before starting her own business. For a time the family lived in Amman in Jordan, where Michael Middleton worked with the airline, but for the most part Catherine and her younger sister and brother were raised in Berkshire, England. She went to the prestigious Marlborough College then took a year out to travel and study at the British Institute in Florence before enrolling at St Andrews to study history of art.

After Eton, Prince William had also taken a gap year, but his travels included a jungle training exercise with the Welsh Guards in Belize

Theresa May: Leading the United Kingdom Out of Europe

When David Cameron tendered his resignation to the Queen on 13 July 2016, the Queen contemplated that she would have a woman as her prime minister for only the second time in her 64 years on the throne. More than a quarter of a century after Margaret Thatcher had been forced out of office, Theresa May became leader of the Conservative Party and Britain's prime minister.

Theresa Mary May (née Brasier) was born in Eastbourne, Sussex, on 1 October 1956, although she was brought up in Oxfordshire, where her father was the vicar of St Mary's Church in Wheatley. Theresa Brasier went to Holton Park Girls' Grammar School in Wheatley before studying geography at Oxford University, where she joined the Oxford University Conservative Association. It was through the association that she met her husband, Philip May, now an investment banker, and the couple were married in 1980.

Mrs May worked at the Bank of England and as a financial consultant, before standing for election as the MP for North West Durham in the 1992 General Election. She failed to dislodge the sitting Labour MP, and also failed in the 1994 Barking by-election, but finally became MP for Maidenhead in the 1997 General Election. She held a number of Shadow Cabinet posts from 1998 onwards and was Home Secretary in the 2010 Conservative/Liberal Democrat coalition government under David Cameron. For the first two years of her term as Home Secretary, Mrs May was also Minister for Women and Equalities.

When David Cameron resigned following the referendum on membership of the European Union, claiming that as he had campaigned to remain in the EU he could not lead the country out of Europe, Mrs May won a leadership election and became prime minister. As prime minister, she was the first foreign leader to meet with Donald Trump after his inauguration as President of the USA in January 2017, determined to maintain the "special relationship" between the UK and the US and to pave the way for independent trade deals once Britain had left the EU.

In April 2017 Mrs May called for a General Election in June, hoping to increase the Conservatives' slender majority to give her security ahead of difficult EU departure negotiations. Embarrassingly for Mrs May, the Conservative Party actually lost 13 seats, forcing a working arrangement with Northern Ireland's Democratic Unionist Party to claw back an even smaller majority.

and 10 weeks in Chile working as a teacher with other volunteers on a Raleigh International project. When he began at St Andrews in 2001, the press agreed that, much as they had done during his school days, they would not harass him, one of the prince's concerns having been that his presence at St Andrews might spoil the university experience for other students.

Although he kept a low profile at first, the press largely adhered to their agreement not to harass him while he was at St Andrews and William began to enjoy more of university life. He played rugby, football and water polo, making new friends. In his second year he moved out of halls of residence to share a flat with friends, one of whom was Catherine.

While the world's media devoted countless hours and column inches to the on-off saga of the romance between the beautiful young commoner and the most eligible bachelor prince on the planet, Prince William and Catherine did their best to get on with their lives. When they graduated from St Andrews, Catherine went to work in the family business and William began his military career. As the future commander-in-chief of the armed forces, he was required to gain experience in all arms of the services. He knew that, as second in line to the throne, he would never be permitted to serve in a combat zone but he was determined to do something that would be of use. He eventually opted to train as a Search and Rescue pilot, flying Sea King helicopters with the RAF.

The announcement of the couple's engagement came after they had been on a holiday with friends in Kenya. On 19 October 2010, Prince William presented Catherine with the world-famous sapphire and diamond engagement ring that had belonged to his mother. In interviews the couple gave after the formal announcement the following month, Prince William said that the ring was his way of "making sure that my mother didn't miss out on today" but admitted that he had been as nervous about looking after the ring as he had been about asking Catherine to marry him. "I had been carrying it around with me in my rucksack for about three weeks," he said. "Everywhere I went I was keeping hold of it because I knew that if it disappeared I would be in a lot of trouble."

The wedding date was set for 29 April 2011 and it was to be a spectacular, glittering occasion. As the future king, Prince William's wedding was a state occasion and was attended by guests from around the world, including foreign royalty, Commonwealth governors-general, politicians, diplomats, representatives of the armed forces and religious dignitaries. At the first meeting to plan the occasion, the prince was presented with a list of hundreds of names and was dismayed and alarmed to find that he recognized none of them. He phoned his grandmother for "clarification" on the protocol and later said that she told him that it was "ridiculous" and that he and Catherine should invite their own friends first. In the end, there were 1,900 guests at Westminster Abbey, 600 who attended a lunch at Buckingham Palace and 300 for dinner and dancing in the evening.

Hundreds of thousands lined the streets to watch the wedding processions to and from Westminster Abbey and, with the day having been declared a public holiday, more than 5,000 street parties were held in towns all over Britain. On the morning of the wedding, Prince William was created Duke of Cambridge, Earl of Strathearn and Baron Carrickfergus, meaning that after the ceremony Catherine became Her Royal Highness The Duchess of Cambridge.

When the couple stood on the balcony at Buckingham Palace as man and wife, the crowd at the palace gates roared for the now-traditional kiss, which was beamed and streamed around the world to a global audience that has been estimated at up to two billion.

ENGAGEMENTS AND GREAT-GRANDCHILDREN

Like his older brother, Prince Harry went to Eton but, unlike Prince William, he did not go to university. He spent a gap year working with charities in Africa before he entered the Royal Military Academy Sandhurst in May 2005. He was commissioned into the Blues and Royals, one of the Household Cavalry regiments, in April 2006, nine months before Prince William completed officer training at Sandhurst and was commissioned into the same regiment. Both trained as tank commanders but, while Prince William was forced to accept that he could not be deployed to a war zone, Prince Harry was determined to share the risks of the men with whom he served. When his unit was scheduled to be deployed to Iraq in 2007, extremist groups made specific threats to kill or capture him. The prince threatened to resign his commission if he was not allowed to go but appeared to have been persuaded by the argument that his presence in Iraq would put those around him in even greater danger than they would otherwise face.

Instead of Iraq, it was announced that Prince Harry was to join a training exercise in Canada. The exercise turned out to be preparation for deployment to Afghanistan in late 2007, where the prince secretly spent three months on the front line before the German and Australian press broke the story that he was there and he was recalled. Back in the UK, he trained with Prince William as a helicopter pilot but, while his brother went on to train on Search and Rescue Sea Kings, Prince Harry qualified as an Apache gunship pilot. He returned to Afghanistan with the Army Air Corps in September 2012 for a 20-week deployment. In an interview filmed in Afghanistan for television's *Channel 4 News*, the prince was asked how Prince William felt about him being there. "There is a bit of jealousy, not just that I get to fly this," he said, patting his Apache, "but because he would love to be out here..." He also admitted to being "more soldier than prince" in the way he lived his life, although he knew that, in the not too distant future, his duties as a prince would supersede his role in the army.

Although he remains closely associated with the military, not least through the Invictus Games, Prince Harry left the army in June 2015 and a few months later was introduced, by a mutual friend, to American actress Meghan Markle. The prince was not aware that Meghan starred in the long-running US television legal drama *Suits* and, with the royal family enjoying a lower profile in the USA than at home, Meghan was only vaguely aware of who Prince Harry was. Nevertheless, they found that they had much in common, especially through the separate charity projects with which they had been involved, and over a period of months a romance developed. Buckingham Palace announced their engagement on 27 November 2017. While the royal family had welcomed with open arms the person Prince Harry described in a BBC interview as "this beautiful woman [who] just tripped and fell into my life", there were elements of the press and social media that had not been so kind. A year prior to the engagement, the prince's communications secretary had issued a statement calling for an end to the "wave of abuse and harassment" to which Meghan and her family had been subjected and condemning the "racial undertones" when some reports referred to Meghan's mother being African-American in a less than complimentary fashion. Happily, Prince Harry and Meghan weathered the storm and their wedding was held on 19 May 2018 at St George's Chapel, Windsor.

St George's Chapel was also the venue for the marriage of Prince Andrew's younger daughter, Princess Eugenie. The engagement of the princess to Jack Brooksbank, whom she had been dating for several years, was announced on 22 January 2018. The couple had met when the princess was on a ski holiday in Verbier, Switzerland, and Brooksbank was working in the resort. Brooksbank, three years older than Princess Eugenie, went to the exclusive Stowe School then worked in pubs, restaurants and upmarket nightclubs, ultimately setting up his own company as a wine wholesaler. The couple managed to maintain their romance even when Princess Eugenie moved to work for an auction company in New York for two years, but were able to abandon the "Skype" relationship when she returned to London to become an associate director of the Hauser & Wirth art gallery.

One of the most recent grandchildren to arrive was Lady Louise Windsor, daughter of the Earl and Countess of Wessex, the title taken by the Queen's youngest son, Prince Edward, when he married Sophie Rhys-Jones. Lady Louise was born on 8 November 2003 and was followed by her younger brother James, Viscount Severn, on 11 December 2007. With so many of her grandchildren settling in to married life, the twenty-first century has seen the Queen become a great-grandmother several times over. Peter and Autumn Phillips had daughters Savannah on 29 December 2010 and Isla on 29 March 2012, while Prince Harry lost his spot as third in line to the throne when his nephew, Prince George of Cambridge, was born on 22 July 2013. Zara and Mike Tindall had a daughter, Mia, on 17 January 2014 and Prince George's little sister,

Princess Charlotte, arrived on 2 May 2015, and on 23 April 2018 Prince William and the Duchess of Cambridge welcomed their second son Prince Louis. On 18 June 2018 the Tindalls had a second daughter, Lena, and Prince Harry and the Duchess of Sussex are expecting their first baby in the spring of 2019.

THE FUTURE OF THE MONARCHY

With so many grandchildren and great-grandchildren to support the House of Windsor – although technically Princess Anne's children and grandchildren have no titles and are not "royal" members of the royal family – the future of the family is assured and the future of the monarchy also looks to be set on a positive footing. In the coming years the Queen's children and grandchildren will increasingly shoulder more of the royal family's responsibilities.

In May 2011 the Queen and Prince Philip made a historic visit to the Republic of Ireland, the first time a British monarch had visited the country and the first time a British monarch had set foot in the south since her grandfather, King George V, 100 years before, when the whole of the island of Ireland was still part of the United Kingdom. The Queen helped to cement relations between the Republic and the United Kingdom when she followed a speech by Ireland's President Mary McAleese at a state dinner in Dublin Castle, beginning her address with "President and friends..." in precisely pronounced Irish Gaelic. The courtesy drew gasps and huge applause from the assembled politicians and dignitaries.

In the Republic of Ireland, the Queen proved the diplomatic impact that she can have abroad, although by then she had begun to cut back on her long-haul trips. The last of those was to the Commonwealth Heads of Government meeting in Australia in 2011, with more recent foreign trips being limited to Europe. In 2012, her Diamond Jubilee year, the Queen's children and grandchildren handled the Commonwealth visits that had previously been undertaken by the Queen and Prince Philip for the Silver and Golden Jubilees. Prince Charles and the Duchess of Cornwall toured

Angela Merkel: The Most Powerful Woman in Europe

Since 2004 the influential business magazine *Forbes* has produced a list of the most powerful women in the world. One name has dominated the list – Angela Merkel. Mrs Merkel became Chancellor of Germany in November 2005 and in every year since then bar one (2010, when Michelle Obama topped the list) *Forbes* has judged her to be the world's most powerful woman.

In times past the "most powerful woman" description has been applied to the Queen and, of course, she remains head of the Commonwealth, but that position, although it brings with it a degree of influence, does not confer upon the Queen the sort of power that is wielded by the heads of the multi-national conglomerates and political leaders listed by *Forbes*. Angela Merkel holds the reins of power not only in Germany but also, because of Germany's booming economy, within the institution of the European Union as well.

That institution was in its absolute infancy as the European Coal and Steel Community when Angela Dorothea Kasner was born in Hamburg, West Germany, on 17 July 1954. Her father was a Lutheran pastor and when he was offered a position in Quitzow, East Germany, the family moved to the east when little Angela was only a few months old. At school, she learned to speak Russian and excelled in mathematics, going on to study physics at university in Leipzig in 1973. In 1977 she married scientist Ulrich Merkel, although the marriage ended in divorce in 1982.

Mrs Merkel worked as a researcher and was awarded a doctorate after publishing her thesis on quantum chemistry in 1986. She became involved in politics after the fall of the Berlin Wall in 1989 and stood for election in Stralsund-Nordvorpommern-Rügen in the newly reunified Germany in 1990. She has been re-elected to represent the district at every election since. She became the first female leader of a German political party when she was elected leader of the Christian Democratic Union of Germany (CDU) in 2000. The 2005 national election ended in stalemate and Mrs Merkel's CDU, having formed a coalition with the Christian Social Union (CSU), formed a further coalition with their main opposition to finally form a government. With the "Grand Coalition" in place, Mrs Merkel became Germany's first female Chancellor. She was to remain Chancellor through three further elections as the head of resulting coalition governments.

Although Mrs Merkel continues to use the name of her first husband, she married Joachim Sauer, a research scientist at Berlin's Humboldt University, in 1998.

Australia, New Zealand, Papua New Guinea and Canada; Prince William and the Duchess of Cambridge were in the Solomon Islands and Tuvalu; Prince Harry went to the Bahamas, Belize and Jamaica; Prince Edward and the Countess of Wessex were in Barbados and the Caribbean islands.

The Queen and Prince Philip travelled throughout the UK and were present at the official celebrations when the traditional spring bank holiday was moved to Monday 4 June and an extra bank holiday was declared on Tuesday 5 June, creating a four-day Diamond Jubilee weekend. The celebrations manifested themselves in a variety of ways. There were the traditional street parties and parades all over the country, but there was also extensive planting of trees, with 40,000 planted on Derbyshire's Chatsworth Estate alone, and volunteers pledged more than two million hours of community work for the "Jubilee Hour". The Olympic park in East London where the 2012 Olympic Games were to be held was officially named the Queen Elizabeth Olympic Park and the clock tower that is home to the Big Ben bell at the Houses of Parliament was renamed the Elizabeth Tower.

One of the highlights of the Jubilee weekend was the Thames Jubilee River Pageant when the royal family watched from a specially commissioned Royal Barge as a fleet of 670 vessels – military, commercial and pleasure craft of all shapes and sizes – paraded down the river in a procession that stretched for seven-and-a-half miles (12.1 kilometres).

Prince Philip missed some of the celebrations through illness – and at 91 years of age he could be excused for beginning to look a little less robust than the young naval officer who had become the Queen's consort in 1952. By the time he and the Queen celebrated their 70th wedding anniversary (the Platinum Wedding) in November 2017, Prince Philip had decided to step down from public life. The Queen said in her Christmas broadcast, "I don't know that anyone had invented the term 'platinum' for a 70th wedding anniversary when I was born. You weren't expected to be around that long." She also quoted Prince Philip as saying that he had "done his bit".

Retirement may never be an option for the Queen. She will never set aside the vow that she made in her 21st birthday broadcast from South Africa that her "whole life, whether it be long or short, shall be devoted to your service", but there has been speculation that when she reaches the age of 95 she may appoint Prince Charles as Prince Regent, meaning that most of the burden of the monarch's duties would become his responsibility. Just as the Queen has reigned longer than any other British monarch, Prince Charles has been heir apparent and Prince of Wales longer than any other.

The next generation is also preparing itself to take on the highest-profile royal roles. The Queen's grandchildren have involved themselves with charities, social projects and humanitarian work that mean most to them. Prince William and Prince Harry carried forward their mother's support for charities working with HIV and AIDS victims as well as the eradication of landmines but have since expanded their interests into a number of different areas. In 2009 they set up an umbrella organization and in 2012 they renamed it The Royal Foundation of the Duke and Duchess of Cambridge and Prince Harry. The aim of the foundation is, where appropriate, to co-ordinate the efforts and maximize the impact of the wide range of charities with which they are involved. Prince William described the foundation as providing "a unique opportunity for us to use our privileged position to make a real difference in the future".

Plans and preparations are almost certainly being put in place for the way that the monarchy will evolve, making it an institution that is set firm for the future. Just as King George V and Queen Mary took steps to secure the monarchy by establishing the House of Windsor a century ago, the younger members of that house now seem determined that it should stand for another century and beyond.

INDEX

Page references in **bold** refer to main entries; page references in *italic* refer to photographs//captions

Burgess, Guy 95
Bush, George W. 118

Cairncross, John 95
Callaghan, James 92
Callender, Alex 89
Calypso, HMS 18
Cameron, David 205
Camilla, Duchess of Cornwall 104, 110,
    114, 115, 120–1
Canberra, RMS 102
Carter, Jimmy 92
Castro, Fidel 55
Catherine, Duchess of Cambridge 59, 123,
    125–6, 129, 131
Chamberlain, Neville 31, 69
Changing of the Guard 103
Charles I of Austria 16
Charles, Prince, Prince of Wales 6, 42, 68,
    79, 80, 81, 86, 87, 93
    affair 115
    Diana's death 115, 116, 117
    education 79, 80
    marries Camilla 120–1
    marries Diana 59, 104–5, 106
    honeymoon 122
    investiture 81, 88
    mentor 81, 93
    as Prince Regent 132
    separation and divorce 109–10, 115
Charlotte Elizabeth, Princess 129
Children's Hour 35
children's rights 3
Christian IX 14
Christmas broadcasts iv, 35, 61, 62, 64,
    87–8, 118, 131
Church of England 22, 70, 121
Church of Scotland 121
Churchill, Lord Randolph 31
Churchill, Sir Winston 12, 19, **31**, 32, 34,
    36, **37**, **44–5**, 47, 63, 69, 70, 84
Clarence House 42, 51, 105
Classiebawn Castle 93
Cold War 28, 41, 52, 65–6, 75, 76, 97
Collingwood, HMS 23
Colville, Richard 66
Commonwealth v, 23, 26, 35, 40, 50, 53, 54
    political power struggles 82
    tours 61–8, 90
Connors, Jane 66
constitutional crises 16, 20–3, 70
coronations 21, 26, **51**, **53–4**, 71
Cox, James M. 27
Crawford, Marion ("Crawfie") 25, 30
Crystal Palace 87
Cuban Missile Crisis 55, 76, 78

D-Day 34, 52
"Dad's Army" 32

Dalton, Canon John 6
Darwon, Harry 65
de Gaulle, Charles **46**, 91
devolution 121
Diana: Her True Story (Morton) 109–10
Diana, Princess of Wales 96, 97, 114–15
    death 115
    marries 59, 97, 104–6, 109–10
    funeral 116, 117
    honeymoon 122
    separation and divorce 109–10, 111
    voice coaching 114, 115
Díaz-Balart, Mirta 55
Dimbleby, David 115
Douglas-Home, Sir Alex 84
The Downing Street Years (Thatcher) 100
Dublin Castle 129
Dudley Ward, Freda 22, 24
Duke of Edinburgh *see* Philip, Prince, Duke
    of Edinburgh
Dumfries House v
Dunkirk 32
Durham, Lord 18
Durham Miners' Union 12

Eagle, HMS 68
Eden, Anthony 69, 72
Edmonds, Pete 90
Edward Albert, Prince ("David"), Prince of
    Wales *see* Edward VIII
Edward Antony, Prince, Earl of Wessex
    79, 80–1, 88, 105, **119–20**, 128
Edward, Duke of Windsor *see* Edward VIII
Edward George, Prince, Duke of Kent 47
Edward VII 4–6, 7, 14
Edward VIII 20–3, 25, 30, 56, 81, 121
    abdication 19–23
    accession 21, 22
    as Duke of Windsor 45, 47
    as Prince of Wales 21, 22
Eisenhower, Dwight D. 52, 55, 78
Elizabeth Alexandra ("Lilibet"), Princess *see*
    Elizabeth II
Elizabeth, Duchess of York *see* Queen
    Mother
Elizabeth II 24, 35, 38, 40, 68
    accession 44, 45, 50, 51
    assassination attempts 97–9
    birth 24, 34
    in British Army 34, 36, 57
    Charles's second wedding 121
    children's births 42, 79
    coronation 51, 53–4, 71
    Diana's death 115, 116
    45th wedding anniversary 110
    George VI's death 44–5, 49–50, 62
    Golden Wedding anniversary 113–14
    "little interlude" 66–7
    marries 40, 42, 58

C R E D I T S

The publishers would like to thank the following sources for their kind permission to reproduce the pictures in this book.

P56 (top) Hughes & Mullins/Hulton Archive/Getty Images, p56 (bottom) Gamma-Keystone via Getty Images, p57 (top) Bettmann/Getty Images, p 57 (bottom) Central Press/Hulton Archive/Getty Images, p58 (top) Popperfoto/Getty Images, p58 (bottom) Rolls Press/Popperfoto/Getty Images, p59 (top) Tim Graham/Getty Images, p59 (bottom) John Stillwell - WPA/Getty Images, p60 (top) Mark Cuthbert/UK Press via Getty Images, p60 (bottom) Anwar Hussein/Getty Images

Every effort has been made to acknowledge correctly and contact the source and/or copyright holder of each picture and Carlton Books Limited apologizes for any unintentional errors or omissions, which will be corrected in future editions of this book.